THE GOSPEL OF THE LORD

Francis J. Moloney, S.D.B.

THE GOSPEL OF THE LORD

Reflections on the Gospel Readings
Year A

A Liturgical Press Book

Scripture quotations are taken from *The Jerusalem Bible* version of the gospels, copyright 1966, 1967 and 1968 by Darton, Longman & Todd (London) and Doubleday & Company (New York). This is the text used, with permission, in *Lectionary I, Proper of Seasons, Sundays in Ordinary Time* (London: Collins/Geoffrey Chapman, 1981).

Cover design by Greg Becker.

First published in 1992 by St. Paul Publications, Homebush, Australia.

Published in the United States of America and Canada by The Liturgical Press, Collegeville, Minnesota 56321. Printed in the United States of America.

1 2 3 4 5 6 7 8 9

Library of Congress Cataloging-in-Publication Data

Moloney, Francis J.
The Gospel of the Lord : reflections on the Gospel readings : Year A / Francis J. Moloney.
p. cm.
Originally published: Homebush, Australia : St. Paul Publications, 1992.
Includes bibliographical references.
ISBN 0-8146-2268-2
1. Bible. N.T. Matthew—Sermons. 2. Sermons, English. 3. Catholic Church—Sermons. 4. Bible. N.T. Matthew—Meditations. 5. Lectionary preaching—Catholic Church.
BS2575.4.M59 1995
251—dc20 95-7431
CIP

For Nerina

CONTENTS

PREFACE

Brief commentaries and reflections upon the Sunday Gospels for Year A of the Liturgical Year form the heart of this book. They have their origins in *The Saving Word*, a weekly publication of the Society of St Paul in Australia used at many Sunday Parish Liturgies. This book presents an expanded version of these reflections with the hope that they will be of use to those who preach and listen to the Sunday Gospel. They are written with both audiences in mind.

I have opened this reflection on Year A with a general introduction to the Gospel of Matthew and an indication of the use the Lectionary makes of this Gospel over the Ordinary Sundays of the year. I provide these two introductory chapters to direct my reader, through the Sunday Lectionary, towards a deeper understanding of Matthew's Gospel. One of the great riches of the Christian tradition which is least appreciated by Christians in general is the four-fold Gospel tradition. So many of us simply speak and think of 'the Gospel', rather than 'the four Gospels'. The three year cycle of the Sunday readings provides an excellent opportunity for Christians to become more familiar with each of the synoptic Gospels (Matthew [Year A], Mark [Year B] and Luke [Year C]), and it was designed for that purpose. In order to provide some guidance for every eventuality over the course of a liturgical year, I have also added commentaries for the Gospels proper to other Feasts which may occur on a Sunday.

At times the translation of the New Testament at present in the Lectionary *(The Jerusalem Bible)* lacks sensitivity to the possibilities of inclusive language. This problem is sometimes present in my reflections on the Gospel of Matthew, as I have attempted to write texts which reflect the passage read in the Liturgy. Mainstream Christian theology and preaching continue to use the male biblical terminology of God as Father and Jesus as Son, but I have attempted to soften such language wherever possible. I apologise in advance for any offence in this delicate area, asking that my respect for the texts as they are found in the Lectionary and Christianity's traditional biblical language and imagery be understood as the reason for certain expressions. In the general study of the Gospel of Matthew which opens this book, I have avoided the text of *The Jerusalem Bible*. With the help of the *Revised Standard Version* and the *New Revised Standard Version*, I have attempted to use the biblical text in a more inclusive fashion.

I am grateful to Michael Goonan, SSP, who suggested and encouraged the publication of these reflections in this form. I am also grateful to another member of the Pauline family, Nerina Zanardo, FSP. She carefully read through the original commentaries and made further suggestions which developed and enriched the original short columns from *The Saving Word*.

I am dedicating this volume of *The Gospel of the Lord* to Nerina, my long-standing and loyal friend. Her gracious presence to the world of Christian book production and marketing in this country over many years, and especially since she has been the Provincial of the Daughters of St Paul in Australia, is a wonderful witness to the spirit of her founder and the dream of her Religious Congregation.

Francis J. Moloney, SDB

Salesian College
Chadstone
Victoria 3148 Australia
23rd March 1992

THE GOSPEL OF MATTHEW

The Gospel readings for Year A in the Lectionary are dominated by an almost continuous reading of the Gospel of Matthew. This is particularly the case for the Ordinary Sundays of the Year, but when the Church has a choice for the other Liturgical Seasons, it regularly chooses a suitable reading from the Gospel of Matthew. This fact calls for thought and comment.

Why does the Church look back to this ancient text and read it thoroughly throughout the course of a Liturgical Year? It is not enough to affirm that the Gospel of Matthew is a part of our inspired Bible, and therefore should be read. How did it find its way into the Bible? There were many other gospels written in the early years of the Church. Something about the Gospel of Matthew gave it authority in the early Church, and still addresses the Church's life and Liturgy. The test of the relevance of any story lies in its capacity to speak to the experience of readers of any place and time. The practice of reading the Gospel of Matthew over the centuries indicates that this ancient story of Jesus has passed that test.

This first chapter attempts to present something of the uniqueness of Matthew's story of Jesus, to see how this version of the life, teaching, death and resurrection of Jesus has spoken and still speaks to the experience of Christian readers. Our reaching back over nearly two thousand years, to touch again the narrative design and the message of an ancient text must not be an exercise in history or archeology. If it is only that, we merely find ourselves in touch with yet another ancient text.

Our approach to the Gospel of Matthew must be made with an important question in our minds. Can this text, which was written to address a Jewish-Christian Church in the '80s of the first century, still be a word of life for us in the 1990s? The commentaries on the Gospel readings from the Sunday Lectionary for Year A which form the heart of this book should not be read as a series of reflections upon unrelated texts. The Gospel of Matthew as a whole has its plot, and this plot was designed to address a readership both in its single parts, and as a whole utterance. While the commentaries forming the major part of this book focus attention upon the single parts, the survey of the Gospel of Matthew which follows attempts to identify the point of view communicated by the whole utterance of this story of the life of Jesus. First, I will draw attention to the major theological themes developed by the author of the Gospel of Matthew. Then, with these themes in mind, I will show how the story of the Gospel, from 1:1-28:20, has a design, a plot that communicates the author's point of view to the reader.

A starting point: Matthew 28:16-20

Strange as it may seem, all biblical scholars recognise that the most logical place to begin a search for the purpose and message of the Gospel of Matthew, its 'point of view', is at its conclusion. In Mt 28:16-20 the risen Jesus gathers his disciples on a mountain in Galilee and sends them out to the whole world. A good story often reaches its climax on the last page. The Gospels are no exception to this (see, for example, Lk 24:44-48; Jn 20:30-31). The Matthean community understood itself and its apostolic task in terms of the commission given by the risen Lord. This commission is explicitly stated in 28:16-20. It is so important that we will consider this text in some detail. This passage runs as follows:

> Now the eleven disciples went to Galilee, to the mountain to which Jesus had directed them. And when they saw him they worshipped him; but some doubted. And Jesus came and said to them: 'All authority in heaven and on earth has been given to me. Go therefore and make disciples of all nations, baptising them in the name of the Father and of the Son and of the Holy Spirit, teaching them to observe all that I have commanded you; and lo, I am with you always, to the close of the age' (Mt 28:16-20).

After the Easter events (see Mt 28:1-15), the disciples return to Galilee, to the mountain indicated by Jesus (v. 16). This is not the first time that Jesus has summoned his disciples to the top of a mountain to give them important instructions. Earlier in the Gospel (5:1-7:28) he began his ministry of teaching by gathering his disciples on a mountain (see 5:1) to give them a New Law (see 5:17-20, 21-22, 27-28, 31-32, 33-34, 38-39, 43-44). On a new Sinai a new and perfect Moses gives a New People of God a New Law. As the situating of the giving of the New Law on a mountain was important, so is it also important for the risen Lord's commissioning of his Church.

Both uses of a mountain, of course, have their origins in the importance of mountains, beginning with Sinai, in the biblical tradition (see Ex 19). We are about to witness a significant communication of God's ways and teaching to the disciples. One senses a community well-versed in, and full of respect and appreciation for, the traditional religious symbols of Israel behind these indications. Yet, as we will see, the details of the commission of Jesus to his disciples appear to contradict that respect and appreciation.

The reaction of the disciples to the sight of Jesus is ambiguous. Some worship him. The Greek verb used here *(proskunein)* is used extensively in the Gospel of Matthew to show a correct understanding of who Jesus is and how one should relate to him (see, for example, Mt 2:2, 11; 4:9-10; 8:2; 9:18; 14:33; 15:25; 18:26; 20:20; 28:9, 17). But despite the fact that some of the disciples worship Jesus, and despite the climactic significance of this final scene, Matthew still reports: 'but some doubted' (v. 17). The hesitation of the disciples in the presence of the risen Lord, one of the hallmarks of all the synoptic resurrection accounts (see Mk 16:8, 9-11, 14 and Lk 24:10-11, 13-35, 36-37), is also an important part of Matthew's theology of the Church. All the Gospels have a realistic understanding and presentation of disciples of Jesus. They believe, yet they falter in their belief.

Jesus opens his final instructions with a declaration about himself, and then spells out the consequences of such a declaration for his disciples and their mission. The man whom they had known as Jesus of Nazareth claims that all authority on heaven and earth has been given to him (v. 18). This is nothing less than to claim that Jesus has taken over the authority and dignity which traditional Israel allowed only to YHWH. Passages which indicate this are innumerable. An example, and perhaps the most important Old Testament passage on the oneness of God and his complete authority, is found in Deut 6:4-9 which begins: 'Hear, O Israel, the Lord is our God, the Lord alone' (Deut 6:4). Behind Jesus' claims to absolute authority there is probably also a reference to the giving of all authority to the 'one like a son of man' in Dan 7:14: 'To him was given, dominion and glory and kingship, that all peoples, nations and languages should serve him'.

On a mountain with his hesitant disciples, Jesus claims to have been given all the authority which, according to traditional Judaism, belonged to YHWH alone. This is a bold claim. It would not have been well received by the Jews of the 80's of the first century. After the destruction of the Temple-city Jerusalem and Israel as a political entity in 70 AD, Judaism had to struggle through a period of religious reconstruction. The Jews no longer had a capital city with its Temple; they no longer had a Land. Judaism gradually established its identity after the disastrous effects of the Jewish war of 70 AD by developing what had once been the Judaism of the Pharisees in the pre-70's period, into a universal (although still varied) way of approaching YHWH, the unique and traditional God of Israel, which came to be called Rabbinic Judaism. It was broadly based on the synagogue as a place of worship and upon the Law as a way of life.

Within this religious context, Matthew's Gospel develops a very exalted idea of Jesus. The profound understanding of Jesus, to whom all authority in heaven and on earth has been given, reflected in Mt 28:17, is paralleled only by some of the christological claims of the Fourth Gospel (see, for example, Jn 5:17-18, 10:30). Over against the synagogue's attempts to re-establish YHWH and his Law at the centre of post-war Judaism, this Gospel presents Jesus as having been given the authority and privilege allowed only to YHWH.

Flowing from the uniqueness and universality of his authority, the Matthean Jesus then breaks through three further elements basic to post-70AD Rabbinic Jewish belief and practice.

(1) He commands his disciples to 'Go therefore and make disciples of *all nations*' (v. 19a). This is in direct opposition to the belief in Israel's exclusive place among the nations of the world as God's chosen people. Once again, this would have been hard for post-war Rabbinic Judaism to accept. Although there had been an openness to the idea of a universal salvation in the prophets (see, for example, Is 2:1-4), it had always meant a movement from the Gentile world towards Sion. Here this is reversed: the new people of God, founded by Jesus of Nazareth, is to 'go out' to make disciples of all nations.

(2) The disciples are further instructed to 'baptise' in the name of the Father and of the Son and of the Holy Spirit (v. 19b). A new initiation rite is introduced for the new people of God, setting out on its mission. It is to replace the centrally important Jewish rite of circumcision. The Rabbis insisted on circumcision as the central act of initiation to YHWH's unique people. In seeking an identity, barriers which separate one group from another are important. Initiation rites are fundamental to this separation, and the traditional rite of circumcision provided it. But the Christian missionary is told to replace the initiation of circumcision with baptism.

(3) As if what had been commanded so far was not enough, the final command demolishes the very basis of traditional Jewish faith, built upon the teaching and the learning of the Torah. The Torah had become even more central for Rabbinic Judaism. Without the Temple with its priesthood and its cultic actions, Torah alone remained as the heart of the Rabbis' understanding of God's ways among his people and his peoples' approach to him. But even the Torah is replaced. Jesus uses words commonly found in passages on the importance of the Torah: 'to teach', 'to observe', 'commandments' (see, for example, Deut 5-6, esp 6:1, where all these terms appear) to indicate a new teaching: 'teaching them to observe all that I have commanded you' (v. 20a). No longer does the command to teach and observe look to the Torah, but to the teaching of Jesus. The Law of Moses has been replaced by the teaching of Jesus.

Jesus' final words are not words of departure, but words assuring that he will always be with his disciples (v. 20b). In the Gospel of Luke the idea of an ascension is a pictorial image of Jesus actually leaving this earth and returning to his Father but in Matthew there is no trace of any such event. In fact, one could say that the opposite is the case. Matthew's Gospel ends with Jesus' promise that he will never leave them. Of course, *theologically*, one can point out that Luke is saying exactly the same thing through his message of a return to the Father and his eventual sending of the Spirit. But whether it is Jesus' Spirit sent by the Father (Luke) or the abiding presence of Jesus who will never leave his Church (Matthew), the message of God's purposes to found and sustain a holy people in and through Jesus rings true.

From these last few verses of the Gospel of Matthew (28:16-20), one could argue that we are dealing with a Gospel that is extremely hostile to the traditional ways of Judaism, especially as they were being forged in the post-70AD situation of emerging Rabbinic Judaism. They could be read as the charter of a Christian Church which has broken definitively from its origins in Judaism. We are clearly in touch with a community being strongly exhorted to set out on a journey away from the confines of Israel into the new world of a universal Church where Jesus, his ways and his teachings are to be the measure of one's 'belonging'. But from these first indications should we conclude that the traditions of Israel are now a thing of the past, valueless? This would be a partial and thus incorrect reading of the Gospel of Matthew as a whole.

A strange contradiction

Matthew's Gospel is often regarded as the most Jewish of all Gospels. How can it be that the author disregards all that is traditional and sacred to Judaism? Is Matthew's Gospel only concerned with the new? What is the author's attitude to the old, the ways of God in the history of Israel?

Matthew 28:16-20 is found at the end of the Gospel. Matthew's story of Jesus concludes with the sending of the disciples into the Gentile mission, a mission to all the nations. Naturally, tension between the missionary Church and the historical origins of Christianity from within Judaism will be sensed. But there is an equally important passage much nearer the beginning of the story of Jesus:

> Think not that I have come to abolish the Law and the Prophets; I have not come to abolish them, but to fulfil them. For truly, I say to you, till heaven and earth pass away, not an iota, not a dot will pass from the Law until all is accomplished (Mt 5:17-18).

In the light of 28:16-20 we seem to be faced with a strange contradiction. The Gospel concluded in a way that indicated a radical breach between the Christian Church setting out on a mission to all the nations and Israel; but these words of Jesus, as he begins his preaching, mark a close bond between them.

The matter becomes even more complex as we read further into the Gospel. There are two occasions during his public ministry when Jesus speaks about the exclusiveness of his mission to Israel where he similarly limits his disciples' mission to Israel alone. In the light of the universalism of the missionary command in 28:16-20 they are very puzzling.

At the beginning of a long discourse which deals with the mission of the Church, we read:

> These twelve Jesus sent out, charging them: 'Go nowhere among the Gentiles, and into no town of the Samaritans, but go rather to the lost sheep of the house of Israel' (10:5-6).

Some time after this discourse, he responds to the pleas of a Canaanite woman, that he heal her daughter: 'I was sent only to the lost sheep of the house of Israel' (15:24).

These passages from the public ministry of the Matthean Jesus appear to limit the mission of Jesus and his disciples to Israel (10:5-6; 15:24), and exhort the followers of Jesus to live and teach the traditional law of Israel (5:17-18). How can we reconcile this with the boldness of the thrust into the Gentile mission which is at the heart of the risen Lord's closing mandate (28:16-20)?

The Gospel of Matthew is marked by two points of view. One is open and enthusiastic about the newness of the Christian Church, along with the challenge of the Gentile mission; another presents Jesus and his disciples involved in a mission limited to Israel (10:5-6, 15:24), and a perfect living of the law (5:17-18).

Jesus among the Gentiles

The impression gained from our reflections thus far is only slightly weakened by the two miracles which Jesus performs for Gentiles during his public ministry, one of which I have already mentioned: the curing of the daughter of the Canaanite woman.

In 8:5-13 Matthew reports the story of the healing of the Gentile centurion's servant. Although Jesus cures the servant of a Gentile soldier, the miracle is worked within the context of the lack of belief which Jesus finds in Israel (see 8:1-27), and is used, ultimately as a teaching for Israel:

> Truly, I say to you, not even in Israel have I found such faith. I tell you, many will come from east and west and sit at the table of Abraham, Isaac and Jacob while the sons of the kingdom will be thrown into the outer darkness; there men will weep and gnash their teeth (vv. 10-12).

These words on the lips of Jesus formed part of the experience of the members of the Matthean community.

Respectful of their roots within ancient Jewish traditions, they were now inevitably involved in the Gentile mission. In that situation their experience as Christians corresponded to what Jesus had said. Despite Jesus' personal mission to Israel alone, he had already spoken of the later experience of the Matthean Church itself: refused by 'the sons of the kingdom', but sent on a mission to peoples 'from east and west'. Strangely, it will be those to whom the kingdom had been given who will be cast into darkness, while many 'from east and west' would be seated at the table of Abraham. The Christians in Matthew's community had experienced expulsion from the synagogue, and they were now moving into the Gentile mission. These words of Jesus gave them courage, as they wondered about their historical and religious origins within Judaism, a way of approaching God which had refused Jesus and his followers.

A similar point is made in Mt 15:21-28, the story of the 'Canaanite' woman. At the end of Jesus' encounter with the Gentile woman Jesus explains why this particular woman has been granted her request: 'O woman, great is your faith! Be it done for you as you desire' (v. 28). However, this point is not reached until the woman herself has placed her understanding of herself and her request within the context of Jesus' unique mission to Israel (see vv. 23-27). The greatness of her faith has created an exception which proves the rule! A Gentile is used to instruct the true Israel (the Matthean Church) on authentic faith.

A tension resolved

The apparent contradiction between Jesus' program to fulfil the Jewish Law found at the beginning of the Gospel (5:17-18) and its conclusion where the risen Jesus sends his disciples to all nations (28:16-20) is reinforced by a consideration of the two miracles which Jesus performs for Gentiles (8:5-13; 15:21-28). They may be directed towards Gentiles, but they instruct Israel. Yet the contradiction is, interestingly, a key to understanding the situation of the Matthean community, the Evangelist's appreciation and presentation of Jesus, his mission and the mission of the Church.

An important feature of any narrative is the way the story-teller uses the time-line of the story being told. Sometimes events are reported as they happen in a human story. This means that the events are reported in the order in which they might happen, one logically following the other. This is generally called *narrative time*. In reading through narrative time, the reader moves simply from one event to another, from one day to another, one year to another, until the end of the story is reached.

But sometimes events or words are reported which look back to an earlier happening, throwing light on the story as it is being reported. An example of this can be found in a famous Gospel story which tells of a blind man. Through a series of events, following one another chronologically *(narrative time)*, he is healed, and subsequently interrogated, until he comes to prostrate himself before Jesus and confess that Jesus is the Son of Man (see Jn 9). But, at the start of the story, the reader is told that this man was 'born blind' (see Jn 9:1). The unfortunate past event of his being born blind enables the disciples to ask who must bear the guilt for this man's affliction. This gives Jesus the chance to set the agenda for the whole story: the man's blindness will lead to the revelation of the glory of God (see 9:2-3).

Again, as often happens in a well-written novel, a hint is given of something that will happen in the distant future. Jesus' predictions of his oncoming passion and resurrection (see, for example, Mk 8:31, 9:31, 10:32-34) are excellent examples of this technique. This sort of inserted information creates a sense of expectancy in a reader, who reads on into the events reported in the narrative, waiting for the accomplishment of some future event which has been promisingly (or threateningly) already been mentioned. Such use of time, which looks either backwards into events which happened earlier, or forecasts future events, is generally called *plotted time.*

Focusing our attention on the temporal element in the passages which highlight the contradiction between the accepted ways of Judaism and the new openness to 'all the nations', we notice that the passages which limit Jesus and his disciples' activities to Israel are located at the beginning, and then during the public ministry of Jesus (5:17-18; 10:5-6; 15:24). The mission to 'all the nations' is the final scene of the Gospel (28:16-20). The events of the life of Jesus follow one another in regular succession, from his birth to his death and resurrection *(narrative time).* But the narrative time of the life, teaching, death and resurrection of Jesus is bracketed between two crucial uses of *plotted time.* The passages which appear to contradict one another, Jesus' insistence upon the fulfilment of the Law in 5:17-18 and his final commissioning of the Church to go out to the whole world in 28:16-20, form this bracket.

Let us look again at the programmatic words of Jesus, found at the beginning of the sermon on the mount (5:17-18). The temporal element of these words calls for a closer examination. Although they come at the beginning of Jesus' ministry in the *narrative time* of the story, they contain words which look outside the unfolding time line of the narrative, into the *plotted time* of the future.

> Think not that I have come to abolish the law and the prophets; I have come not to abolish them but to fulfil them. For truly, I say to you, *till heaven and earth pass away,* not an iota, not a dot, will pass from the law *until all is accomplished.*

I have stressed two different expressions in the passage: they are both references to some future 'time'. There is the 'now' of Jesus' preaching during his public ministry *(narrative time)*, but there is a moment 'yet to come' when the present order of things will be changed *(plotted time)*. These expressions refer to a time in the future when the perfection of the law will be completed: 'till heaven and earth pass away . . . until all is accomplished'. When might that future time be? In the light of our general understanding of Jesus' eschatological teaching (still found in Mt 24) we are immediately led to regard these words of Jesus as referring to the end of all time. Indeed, many scholars do read Mt 5:17-18 as a reference to the traditional Jewish notion of the end of time.

This understanding of the future events referred to in 5:17-18, however, renders Mt 28:16-20 very difficult to understand. In 28:16-20 the story-teller reports words of the risen Jesus which once again use plotted time to reach outside the narrated events of the Gospel. The disciples are sent on a mission to the ends of the earth, and Jesus promises that he will be with them till the close of the age. If the future time of 5:17-18 referred to the end of all time the command of Jesus, that the Jewish Law be perfectly observed, would be in force in the Christian Church, as it awaits Jesus' final coming. But the perfect observance of the Jewish Law is abandoned by Jesus himself in 28:16-20 when sends his disciples on a mission in a way which is at variance with the Law.

Although there may have been different points of view within the community, and some of its members may have claimed that the Church must still live under the Law (5:17-18) while others argued that they must go out to all the nations armed only with the teaching of Jesus (28:16-20), the Gospel must be read as a single utterance which made sense to an author. The author does not leave these contradictory understandings of the Christian

Church to stand unresolved in the Gospel. The author has written a story of Jesus to resolve the seeming contradiction. Indeed, that was one of the practical, pastoral reasons for the writing of the Gospel of Matthew. An understanding of the *uniqueness* of this particular Gospel will show that such is the case.

Between Jesus' insistence on the mission to Israel at the beginning and during the course of his public ministry (5:17-18; 10:5-6; 15:24), and his final commission as the risen Lord to the Matthean disciples to go out to the whole world (28:16-20), something happens which dramatically changes the future roles of both Jesus and his disciples. The events from the narrated time of the story which stand as a watershed between the opening of the ministry of Jesus (5:17-18), his continued insistence upon the limitation of his mission to Israel (10:5-6; 15:24), and his final missionary command, are his death and resurrection (chs 26-27).

The words sending the young Church out to the whole world in the service of a new universal Lord, teaching his commandments, come from the lips of the risen Jesus (28:16-20). Something happens in the Matthean story of the paschal events which transforms the ministry of Jesus and his disciples during the life of Jesus and the mission of the Church in the company of the risen Jesus. There are two moments in the Gospel story — in passages found *only* in Matthew — where there are descriptions which could be regarded as 'heaven and earth passing away' (see 5:17-18). The first of these moments is at the death of Jesus:

> From the sixth hour there was darkness all over the land until the ninth hour. The veil of the temple was torn in two from top to bottom; the earth quaked; the rocks were split; the tombs opened and the bodies of many holy men rose from the dead (27:45, 51-53).

The second of these moments is found in the Matthean description of the events surrounding the resurrection of Jesus:

> All at once there was a violent earthquake, for the angel of the Lord, descending from heaven, came and rolled away the stone and sat upon it. His face was like lightning, his robe white as snow (28:2-3).

Heaven and earth are passing away. Matthew has taken some of the imagery which he uses here from the Christian tradition concerning Jesus' death already used by Mark. That Evangelist also reported the tearing of the veil and the darkness at the death of Jesus, along with the whiteness of the robe of the angel at the tomb, although he was a 'young man', not an angel, in Mark 16:5. When the overall context is put together, however, it is obvious that Matthew has changed the scenario considerably. He has drawn upon some traditionally 'apocalyptic' symbols from Jewish thought but he has shifted their timing. The events described: darkening of the skies, splitting of the rocks, earthquakes, lightning, the rising of the dead and the appearance of angels are events which were expected to happen at the final end of all time when YHWH would return as Lord and Judge. Matthew indicates that all these events not only *will happen* at the very end of history, as was held by Jewish traditions, they already *have happened* at the death and resurrection of Jesus.

The *plotted time* involved in the future time indicated by the words of Jesus 5:17-18 ('till heaven and earth pass away . . . until all is accomplished') has now become *narrated time* in the events of the passion. The promise has been fulfilled. Only Matthew's story of the life of Jesus makes this point. This is his way of saying that the death and resurrection of Jesus is a single event which marks the turning point of the ages. It is the paschal mystery of Jesus which alters everything. Yet, as we have seen from the Gospel itself, Matthew is anxious to show that Jesus himself lived out the perfection of the Old Law (for example, read 3:13-17 in the light of what we have just uncovered), as well as becoming, through his death and resurrection, the foundational figure of the New Law.

We would do Matthew an injustice if we did not see the great care he takes to show that Jesus does not abolish the Old Law. Rather, Jesus perfects the Law, not only in what he does, but also in who he is. This is made particularly clear in Mt 1-2. The events of the birth and infancy of Jesus, bridging the time between the former covenant into the days of Jesus are a fulfilment of the promises of old. Almost every scene in the Matthean infancy narrative indicates that the events of Jesus' birth and infancy are 'to fulfil what was said by the prophet . . .' (see 1:22-23, 2:5-6, 15, 17-18, 23). The same theme also flows into the ministry of Jesus (see 3:3; 4:6-7, 14-16). Matthew was convinced that Jesus was the perfection of all the promises of the Old Testament.

The Gospel of Matthew begins in the Old Testament, through the genealogy of Jesus (1:1-17) where God's providential handling of the history of a chosen people is already obvious. Nevertheless, the promise of the Old Testament is fulfilled in the events of the birth and the public life of Jesus. Yet, Jesus appears to be extremely anxious that his life and ministry be the *perfection* of the Old Law. He himself attempts to live the Law perfectly, and he exhorts his followers to do the same.

However, after his death and resurrection, those same followers are instructed to reach out to the Gentile mission, commanded by a new Lord to teach a new Law, to forge a new community with a new initiation rite (28:16-20). This is possible only because the death and resurrection of Jesus are understood by the Gospel of Matthew as the 'turning point of the ages'.

The members of Matthew's Church are caught up in the Gentile mission. Nevertheless, they are still very aware that they are the product of the perfection of the Old Law in the person and teaching of Jesus. As this is the case, the Evangelist can claim that it is his community, the followers of Jesus of Nazareth, who can regard themselves as the 'True Israel'. The synagogue-centred religion of post-war Judaism, which rejected and expelled the followers of Jesus, could not claim to be Israel. God's saving history, from Abraham to Jesus (see 1:1-17) into the Gentile mission (28:16-20) was being lived out by the Christian Church. The historical Israel had lost its way, and the true Israel was to be located in the missionary Church, the continuation of Jesus' perfection of the Law, transformed by the turning point of his death and resurrection.

The plot of Matthew's Gospel

With this underlying understanding of the way God has acted through Jesus for the perfection of Israel and the bringing of Jesus' saving teaching to the ends of the earth, I will now consider how the plot of Matthew's Gospel, from 1:1 to 28:20 unfolds. The whole utterance of Matthew's Gospel can be read as a single story. It was written to communicate a point of view which is best understood through an analysis of its plot. The plot of this Gospel can be descibed as the way the author has told the words and actions of Jesus, and the order in which they are told, so that a desired impact might be made upon the reader.

One of the features of the Gospel of Matthew is the presence of five lengthy discourses in the story of Jesus (5:1-7:28: the sermon on the mount; 10:1-11:1: the missionary discourse; 13:1-53: the parable discourse; 18:1-35: the discourse on Church life and order; 24:1-25:46: the discourse on the end of time and the final judgment). Many scholars have taken the discourses as the main indication of the internal structure of the Gospel. Such a structure, however, fails to give sufficient attention to the blending of the the discourses with the narratives of

Jesus' infancy, his preaching and healing, his instruction of disciples, his passion, death and resurrection.

Recent interest in the Gospel of Matthew as a narrative with an identifiable plot has shown that the discourses, although important, form part of larger narrative blocks. Depending upon a recent study of F.J. Matera ('The Plot of Matthew's Gospel', *The Catholic Biblical Quarterly* 49 [1987] 233-253), I would like to propose the following design of the narrative of this Gospel, in the hope that it will serve as a guide to a more fruitful reading of the text itself. I would strongly encourage any reader to accompany the reading of the following pages with an attention to the pages of the Gospel of Matthew in order to see the gradual unfolding of the plot as it is found in the text itself.

My explanation of the seeming contradiction which exists between the beginning (5:17-18) and the end (28:16-20) of the Gospel of Matthew leads me to conclude that this Gospel has something to do with:

1. a history of God's saving plan, begun in the promises to Israel, perfected in the life and ministry of Jesus. His death and resurrection marked a turning point in that history, and from that moment on the Church has been sent out, as the true Israel, to the ends of the earth.
2. the presentation of Jesus' identity as the Messiah, the Son of God. This understanding of Jesus is rejected by traditional Israel.
3. the rejection of Jesus by Israel, and the establishment of the true Israel in the Church.
4. the commissioning of the Church to preach the Gospel to the Gentiles.

At the heart of the unfolding plan and argument of the Gospel stand Jesus' death and resurrection as the turning point of the ages, and the great commission which sends the Church into the Gentile mission.

However, these theological themes are embedded in a plot, and plots are formed by a series of narrative units marked by a central scene which is the focus of the unit (sometimes called 'the kernel'), surrounded, supported and further explained by other narratives (sometimes called 'satellites'). The overarching theme of each narrative unit can be gleaned from the major thrust of the key episode and the way in which other episodes flow from it, further explain it and are dependent upon it. But narrative units are never self-contained ends unto themselves. They also contain crisis moments which lead the reader further into the story. There are always hints in the unit which look forward to the end of the story. In a good story the reader is told enough to be made curious, without ever being given all the answers. Narrative texts keep promising the reader the great prize of understanding — later.

On the basis of these simple principles for the understanding of the gradually emerging plot of a narrative, the story line of the Gospel of Matthew can be divided into six units.

1. The first narrative unit: The coming of the Messiah (1:1-4:11)

The kernel of this unit is the birth of Jesus (2:1a). In a unit which makes its central theme the *coming* of the Messiah, his birth is crucial, no matter how briefly the event is mentioned. Indeed, the physical birth of Jesus is only alluded to, rather than described, in 2:1a. Nevertheless, it is the foundation for what precedes: the genealogy of Jesus (1:1-17) and the description of how his birth came about (1:18-25); and the foundation for what follows: the coming of the Wise Men from the East and Israel's response (2:2-12), the flight into Egypt, the slaying of the innocents and the return from Egypt, which leads to a further flight to Nazareth (2:13-23), the preaching of John the Baptist (3:1-12), the baptism of Jesus (3:13-17), and, finally, the temptation of Jesus (4:1-11).

The genealogy (1:1-17) indicates that the birth of Jesus is the fulfilment of God's promises, and this is further strengthened in the annunciation to Joseph (1:18-25). Without this event the story cannot begin and 1:1-25 prepare for such a beginning. Although the appearance of John the Baptist (3:1-12), the baptism of Jesus (3:13-17), and the temptations in the wilderness (4:1-11) occur several years later, they are dependent upon Jesus' coming. Because Jesus of Nazareth (see 2:23) has been born, because he has come, the question can now be asked: is he the Messiah or not? John testifies that he is (3:11, 14). God proclaims that Jesus is his beloved son (3:17). Satan tests Jesus to see if he is God's son (4:1-11).

From the beginning of the story several events foreshadow the ultimate outcome of the plot. The identification of Jesus as 'the son of David, the son of Abraham' (1:1) suggests that the Jewish Messiah will have meaning for all Abraham's children, Jew and Gentile (see Gen 12:1-4). The homage of the Magi (2:11) points to the coming of the Gentiles, as does John's warning to the Pharisees and the Sadducees that 'God is able from these stones to raise up children to Abraham' (3:9). On the other hand, Jerusalem's inability to accept what the Scriptures proclaim, that the Messiah will come from Bethlehem, and Herod's persecution of the infant King of the Jews prefigure the passion. Satan's messianic temptations show that Jesus' messiahship will be misunderstood in terms of power and authority (see the mockery found in the passion story 27:39-44 where many of the terms used by Satan re-appear). Thus the birth of Jesus (2:1a) initiates a crisis in Israel that will not be resolved until Jesus' death and resurrection.

2. *Second narrative unit: The Messiah's ministry to Israel of preaching, teaching and healing (4:12-11:1)*

The kernel of this unit is found in 4:12-17 which describes the beginning of Jesus' ministry. The arrest of John the Baptist (4:12) leads Jesus to withdraw to Galilee and begin his mission (4:12-17), limited exclusively 'to the lost sheep of the house of Israel' (10:6). No longer is Jesus a figure in the background. He is actively present to the story, preaching: 'Repent, for the kingdom of heaven is at hand' (4:17). This section of the Gospel contains the beginnings of Jesus' ministry in Galilee (4:12-25), the discourse of the sermon on the mount (5:1-7:28), a series of nine miracles, separated by brief episodes, all of which are related to the vocation of a disciple of Jesus (8:1-9:38) and the discourse on the mission of the disciples (10:1-11:1).

The entire section is marked by Jesus' messianic ministry of preaching, teaching and healing. This theme is repeated several times in the narrator's commentaries upon his story, at the beginning, in the middle, and at the end of the section: 'And he went about all Galilee, teaching in their synagogues and preaching the gospel of the kingdom and healing every disease and every infirmity among the people' (4:23. See also 9:35; 11:1). He preaches and teaches through the sermon on the mount (5:1-7:28) and his discourse on mission (10:1-11:1). Between the two discourses he works a series of nine miracles to show that he is mighty not only in word but also in deed (8:1-9:38). In brief narratives located between the nine miracle stories, he associates disciples with his ministry of teaching, preaching and healing (8:14-22; 9:9-17; 9:35-38). Jesus has compassion for the crowds, 'harassed and helpless, like sheep without a shepherd' (9:36), and he invites his disciples to pray the Lord of the harvest to send labourers into the harvest (9:37).

However, Jesus does not only exhort to prayer. His compassion and his concern that the Gospel of the kingdom be preached leads him to call his twelve disciples, to give them authority to do all the things which he has done so far in the story, and to send them out on a mission 'to the lost sheep of the house of Israel' (10:1-15). In the discourse which follows Jesus describes how they are to behave towards others and towards one another, as they share the mission (10:1-11:1).

Reading this section of the plot carefully, however, shows that, from its very inception, the mission of Jesus to Israel already produces crises. On the one hand the crowds are astonished at Jesus' teaching (7:28-29), and after the healing of a dumb man they are led to say, 'Never was anything like this seen in Israel' (9:33). The disciples respond generously to Jesus' call (4:20-22), and he sends them on his mission (10:1-11:1). But on the other hand, the Pharisees complain that 'he casts out demons by the prince of demons' (9:34), and Jesus suggests that their ethical behaviour is not in line with their teaching (see 5:20). The disciples are warned that their mission, like Jesus' mission, will cause division and hatred (10:16-25, 34-36). The mixed reception which greets the teaching and healing ministry of Jesus already tells the reader that the Messiah may be rejected.

There are also events in this section which foreshadow the ultimate outcome of the plot. The faith of a centurion points to the coming of the Gentiles, and leads Jesus to say: 'I tell you, many will come from east and west and sit at table with Abraham, Isaac and Jacob in the kingdom of heaven, while the sons of the kingdom will be thrown into the outer darkness' (8:11-12). An accusation, levelled at Jesus during his passion (see 26:65), is aimed at Jesus for the first time when he forgives the sins of a paralytic: 'This man is blaspheming' (9:3). Jesus' ministry to Israel will not be accepted.

3. The third narrative unit: The crisis in the Messiah's ministry (11:2—16:12)

After the conclusion of the first phase of Jesus' ministry (4:12-11:1), John the Baptist, still in prison, sends messengers to enquire: 'Are you he who is to come, or shall we look for another?' (11:3). This question hangs over the whole of this narrative unit. 'The Coming One' is an expression used to speak of the Messiah (see 3:11; 21:9). Jesus uses the question of the Baptist to review his ministry so far: people are healed and the good news is preached (see 11:4-5), but John's question raises another problem which Israel must answer. On the basis of Jesus' ministry of preaching, teaching and healing, now amply displayed in the story so far (especially in the previous narrative section, 4:12-11:1) will Israel recognise Jesus as the Coming One, or will Israel be offended by this activity of the Messiah?

A chain of events responds negatively and positively to the question raised by John the Baptist: 'Are you he who is to come, or shall we look for another?' Some will decide that he is the one who is to come, while others will decide, once and for all, that they must look for another. Jesus will take appropriate action in each case. A rift opens between Jesus and traditional Israel, while a close bond between Jesus and his disciples develops. They are the nucleus of the new people of God.

On the negative side, Jesus points to the disappointing reception his ministry has received from 'this generation' (11:6-19) and from the unrepentant cities of Chorazin and Bethsaida (11:20-24). But Jesus then issues an unforgettable invitation: 'Come to me, all who labour and are heavy-laden' (11:28). Jesus offers a yoke and a burden which are easy and light, in contrast to the yoke and the burden of a people who refuse to accept their Messiah. This challenge leads to a series of episodes through which the Pharisees either question or test Jesus authority. The relationship between Jesus and the leaders of Israel is one of anger and distrust (12:1-45), but he establishes a new family of God, not built upon bonds of blood or nation: 'Whoever does the will of my Father in heaven is my brother, and sister, and mother (12:50).

No longer able to speak directly to the crowds, he must turn to a parabolic form of speech, 'because seeing they do not see, and hearing they do not hear, nor do they understand' (13:13). In the parable discourse of 13:1-52 Jesus turns decisively away from Israel, to make himself known to those to whom it has been given to know the secrets of the kingdom of heaven (13:11). After the discourse, as if in answer to his distancing himself from his own people, Jesus is rejected at his home town, Nazareth (13:54-58).

Throughout this section, the Pharisees (sometimes with the scribes) attack Jesus for violating the Sabbath (12:1-14), for casting out demons (12:22-24), and for transgressing the traditions of the elders (15:1-2). They also demand signs (12:38; 16:1). After Jesus cures a blind and a dumb demoniac (12:22), even the crowds ask in disbelief if Jesus can really be the Son of David (12:23).

Positively, Jesus' disciples maintain their faith. Immediately before the parable discourse, he identifies the disciples as his true family (12:48-50). In the parable discourse, he tells them: 'To you it has been given to know the secrets of the kingdom of heaven' (13:11). At the end of the discourse the disciples say they have understood all that Jesus has said, and Jesus identifies them as scribes who have been trained for the kingdom of heaven (13:51-52). But even the faith of the disciples is not perfect. It is described as 'little faith' (14:17). They do not understand the parable about clean and unclean (15:16), and they are annoyed by the Canaanite woman (15:23). But they still confess that Jesus is the Son of God (13:33), and they understand that the leaven of the Pharisees and the Sadducees refers to their teaching (16:12).

A clear line of demarcation is now emerging in the narrative between Israel and its leaders who have become increasingly hostile to Jesus and the believing but fragile disciples who accept and understand him. The story has arrived at a major crisis. Israel is blind to Jesus' teaching, and the religious leaders attack him. Jesus responds by speaking in parables, a speech which Israel cannot understand. As in the narrative section which dealt with Jesus' preaching and healing in Israel, where the storyteller summarised his activity, once again, on three occasions the reader finds that 'Jesus, aware of this, withdrew from there' (12:15. See 14:13a; 15:21). The narrator remarks that Jesus 'withdraws' himself from Israel.

A section of the Gospel (14:1-16:12), highlighted by the two bread miracles of 14:13-21 and 15:32-39, now follows. Jesus deals with his fragile disciples, and their equally fragile leader, Peter (14:22-33). He instructs and argues with the leaders of Israel (15:1-20), and feeds both Israel (14:13-21) and the Gentiles (15:32-39), who have glorified the God of Israel for the miracles he does among them (15:29-31). Jesus has not abandoned Israel and he continues to instruct and nourish the people. However, he increasingly focuses his attention upon his disciples. They are the nucleus of the new nation which will believe in him, and they must be wary of the leaven of the Pharisees and the Sadducees (see 16:1-12).

As in the earlier parts of the Gospel's plot, there are further hints of the end of the story throughout this unit. Jesus is identified with Isaiah's suffering servant (12:17-21), but to the text of Isaiah 42:1-4, 9, the author adds another passage from Isaiah (11:10): 'and in his name will the Gentiles hope' (Mt 12:21). Although initially refusing to reach beyond the boundaries of Israel (15:24), Jesus eventually responds to the requests of the Canaanite woman because of the Gentile woman's great faith (15:28). Because Israel is blind to Jesus' messiahship and the religious leaders attack him, Jesus will turn to all disciples who believe, even Gentiles.

4. The fourth narrative unit: The Messiah's journey to Jerusalem (16:13—20:34)

One of the most quoted, and memorable, of all Gospel stories forms the kernel event which controls this narrative unit. The very first scene is Peter's confession of faith at Caesarea Philippi (16:13-28). In this scene:

i. in response to Jesus' question about public opinion concerning his person, Peter confesses, in the name of the disciples, that Jesus is the Messiah, the Son of God (vv. 13-16).
ii. Jesus announces his death and resurrection (v. 21).
iii. Jesus associates his disciples with his own passion (vv. 23-28).

The previous section of the Gospel (11:2-16:12) struggled with the question raised by John the Baptist: 'Are you the one who is to come' (11:2). The encounter between Jesus, Peter and the disciples provides the answer to John the Baptist's question: Jesus is the Coming One, the Messiah, the Son of God. But this public proclamation of Jesus' messiahship is only half the story. Although there have been hints for the reader that Jesus is destined to be rejected and suffer, the scene at Caesarea Philippi explicitly opens a new direction for the narrative. '*From that time on* Jesus began to show his disciples that he must go to Jerusalem and suffer many things from the elders and the chief priests and the scribes, and be killed, and on the third day be raised' (16:21). The explicit linking of the proclamation of Jesus' messiahship with his suffering produces a further crisis. *From this point on* Jesus' disciples must decide if they can follow a Messiah who calls them to suffering and even death.

The controlling texts in this narrative unit are Jesus' predictions of his passion and resurrection. After the first of these predictions there are a further two passion predictions, strategically placed through this part of the story (17:22-23; 20:17-19). They further develop the key event of Caesarea Philippi by regularly reminding the reader of Jesus' destiny at Jerusalem. However, the reader is not only faced with the information provided by Jesus' regular predictions of his death. The reader also responds to the reaction of the disciples in this section. Although there are encounters with the Pharisees and other characters in the story, they only serve to highlight Jesus' instruction of the disciples, as he calls them to follow their Messiah to a cross. The disciples, in turn, demonstrate that they do not completely understand the nature of Jesus' messiahship and the demands it entails.

The disciples witness, but misunderstand the Transfiguration (17:1-8) and immediately show the littleness of their faith in their inability to cure the epileptic boy (17:14-21). The second prediction of the passion re-orients the narrative towards the cross (17:22-23), and the strange story of the payment of the Temple tax associates Peter with Jesus (17:24-27). The discourse on Church order then follows (18:1-19:1). This detailed discourse on how the community is to treat the sinners and the frail within their midst is created by a question raised by the disciples: 'Who is the greatest in the kingdom of heaven?' (18:1). The Pharisees' question about divorce leads to Jesus' instruction of his disciples on the sacredness of what God has joined together (19:1-12) and the encounter with the rich young man is the springboard for Jesus' instruction of his disciples on wealth and possessions (19:16-30). Throughout, the disciples are taught that, like little children, they must be open and receptive to the ways of God (see 19:13-15).

The counter-cultural nature of this teaching is reinforced by the parable of the master of the vineyard who calls whomever he wishes to work in his vineyard, and whenever he wishes to call them, and pays whatever he decides. After all, he is the Lord of the vineyard (20:1-16). The third passion prediction (20:17-19), however, does not lead to the disciples' conversion to the way of Jesus. The sons of Zebedee, through their mother, seek positions of authority, and when the other ten hear of it, they are indignant (20:20-28). This narrative unit closes with the story of the two blind men who proclaim their faith in Jesus as he comes out of Jericho. Abandoning all because of their belief in him, 'they received their sight and followed him' (20:29-34). The reader, who has followed fragile disciples through this section, learns from the blind men how one should commit oneself to the following of Jesus without any conditions or expectations of human success.

Thus, the event of Caesarea Philippi confronts the disciples with a vision of messiahship and discipleship which they cannot fully integrate at this stage of the story. Nevertheless, the disciples do not abandon Jesus, and he continues to instruct them. At the transfiguration, the Father confirms that Jesus is his beloved son (17:5), and later Jesus explains that Elijah has returned in the person of John the Baptist (17:13). Jesus helps Peter to pay the Temple tax (17:24-27) and then delivers a major discourse on the kind of relationships which should mark his new community (18:1-35). Peter is able to boast that the disciples have left everything in order to follow Jesus (19:27), and Jesus promises that they will sit on 'twelve thrones, judging the twelve tribes of Israel' (19:28). The parable of the workers in the vineyard (20:1-16), which follows this promise, suggests that the disciples are among the last who will be first (19:30; 20:16).

As Jesus approaches Jerusalem, two blind men call him the Son of David (20:30-31). Their confession of Jesus' messiahship, coming at the end of the unit (20:29-34), forms an inclusion with Peter's confession at Caesarea Philippi, which began it (16:13-28). The blind are among the insignificant people who accept Jesus' messiahship. The events of this part of the story lead Jesus to Jerusalem, the city of his destiny. The virtual elimination of the crowd, which only appears incidentally throughout this section of the story (see 17:14; 19:2; 20:29, 31), and the emphasis upon Jesus' teaching the disciples suggests that the disciples will form the nucleus of Jesus' new community, despite their inability to accept completely Jesus' way to resurrection, by means of the cross.

5. The fifth narrative unit: The Messiah's death and resurrection (21:1—28:15)

The kernel event in this section of the Gospel is the cleansing of the Temple. It happens after Jesus enters Jerusalem as its messianic king (see 21:9), and as a consequence of that fact (21:1-17). The event serves as a crisis because it confronts the inhabitants of Jerusalem with the question of Jesus' person and authority. This question played out in the rest of the story, leads inevitably to his final rejection and death on the one hand, but to his victory and resurrection as God's anointed one on the other. Only in Matthew's story of the cleansing of the Temple do the Jewish leaders question Jesus' authority for such outrageous action (see 21:15-16).

The event of the messianic purification of the Temple, powerfully commented upon by the insertion of the destruction of the barren fig-tree, supplies the proximate occasion for Jesus' death. A theme emerges at the cleansing of the Temple which will be repeated on two further occasions as the account draws to its dramatic conclusion. At Jesus' trial, witnesses make the accusation: 'This fellow said, 'I am able to destroy the Temple of God, and to build it in three days'' (26:61). During the crucifixion,

Jesus is mocked: 'You who would destroy the Temple and build it in three days, save yourself!' (27:40). At his death the prophetic gesture of Jesus which began this narrative section becomes a reality: 'And behold, the curtain of the Temple was torn in two, from top to bottom' (27:51).

After Jesus cleanses the Temple, the chief priests and elders of the people ask, 'By what authority are you doing these things, and who gave you this authority?' (21:23). When the religious leaders refuse to answer Jesus' counter-question about the baptism of John, Jesus utters three parables against them (21:28-22:14). In the second of them, he announces that 'the kingdom of God will be taken away from you and given to a nation producing the fruits of it' (21:43).

After the parables the bitter invective against the leaders of Israel continues through a series of controversies with them; with the Pharisees, over the payment of taxes (22:15-22); with the Sadducees, over the resurrection from the dead (22:23-33), and with a Scribe, over the greatest commandment (22:34-40). These debates reduce Jesus' opponents to silence: 'And no one was able to answer him a word, nor from that day did anyone dare to ask him any more questions' (22:46).

As if this were not enough, Jesus next denounces the scribes and Pharisees in a series of seven woes (23:13-36) and pronounces an oracle of doom over Jerusalem (23:37-39). The old world, represented by the established authorities in Israel and the city of Jerusalem, can no longer claim the allegiance of the true people of God: 'The Scribes and Pharisees sit on Moses' seat; so practise and observe whatever they tell you, but not what they do, for they preach, but do not practise' (23:2). Having disposed of the traditional leaders of God's people, Jesus next turns to his disciples, the nucleus of the true people of God. He warns them that they must not be led astray.

Many things must happen before God's plan is ultimately achieved. Jesus foretells the destruction of the Temple and his return as the Son of Man (24:1-51). However, between the 'now' of Jesus' final days with them and the 'end time' when the Son of Man will come in glory, there will be a long 'in between time'. This will be the time of the Church, the new people of God. Therefore, Jesus instructs the disciples to produce works of righteousness during the period of his absence (25:1-46).

The passion opens with a comment from the narrator indicating that the teaching is over, and words from Jesus which look back to his earlier passion predictions. The turning point of the ages has arrived: 'When Jesus had finished all these sayings he said to his disciples, you know that after two days the Passover is coming, and the Son of Man will be delivered up to be crucified' (26:1-2). But the events of the passion of Jesus follow as a result of events initiated by the cleansing of the Temple. Anger and animosity broke out on that occasion which has gone on unabated ever since.

I will not analyse the passion story in any detail. An interested reader might turn to my extended commentary on Mt 26:14-27:66 for Palm Sunday (see below, pp. 96-105). I will limit myself here to an indication of the way the main thrust of the plot is achieved through Matthew's passion. Ironically, Jesus' messianic claims are proclaimed, even by those who condemn him to death. This happens at the Jewish trial, where the messianic terms used at Caesarea Philippi are repeated in the question of the high priest and the response of Jesus: ' "I adjure you by the living God, tell us if you are the Christ, the Son of God". Jesus said to him, "You have said so. But I tell you, hereafter you will see the Son of Man seated at the right hand of Power, and coming on the clouds of heaven" ' (26:63-64). The proceedings of the Roman trial insist that Jesus is 'King of the Jews' (see 27:11, 29) and 'Christ' (27:17, 22).

During the passion the people, who have been fairly passive through all the angry encounters between Jesus and the leaders of Israel, under the influence of their leaders, reject Jesus as the Messiah, and choose a false messianic pretender, Barabbas, in his place (27:15-23). Indeed, they support their demand that Jesus be crucified with terrible words which indicate that the former people of God has made its choice: 'His blood be on us and on our children' (27:25).

But a Gentile soldier and those with him confess that Jesus was truly the Son of God (27:54). In accordance with Jesus' predictions, God raises him on the third day, despite the efforts of the Jewish leaders to make 'the sepulchre secure by sealing the stone and setting a guard' (27:62-66). The fifth narrative unit is the climax of Israel's opposition to the Messiah. As Israel rejects Jesus, the Gentiles in the person of the Roman soldiers begin to accept him. Thus, as the plot moves towards its conclusion, the Gospel moves from Israel to the nations.

6. The sixth narrative unit: The great commission (28:16-20)

This concluding scene stands alone. It is an ending which opens to the future. For the first time, Jesus allows the disciples to teach and to proclaim the Gospel to the Gentiles. Earlier, as we had occasion to see, he limited their mission to the lost sheep of the house of Israel (see 10:5-6; 15:24).

Although the story ends here, the reader knows what will take place after the great commission, thanks to Jesus' parable discourse (13:1-52) and his eschatological discourse (24:1-25:46). In these discourses Jesus tells several parables which explain what will happen in the period between his resurrection and his return as the Son of Man at the close of the age. There will be periods of persecution when many will fall away (13:21). There will be a mixture of good and bad within the Church (13:24-30). Many will grow weary waiting for his return (25:1-13), but at the end of the age Jesus will come as the royal Son of Man to judge the nations (25:31-46). Thus the great commission (28:16-20) is not an ending but a beginning which invites the reader to discipleship and to the evangelisation of the nations.

The experience of the Matthean community

If this is the story of Jesus as it has been told in the Gospel of Matthew, one further question needs to be raised before we begin to read through the Gospel of the Year. Is it possible for us to recapture the experience of the Christian community for which the Gospel of Matthew was written? Given the very clear understanding which the author and his readers appear to have had of the Jewish world and its traditions, the community was obviously largely Jewish in origin. The Jewish background and religious formation of this early Christian community led its members to recognise the greatness of God's ways with his people of old. But it was not only the God of Israel who continued to be at the centre of their belief; they also struggled to somehow understand how they related to the chosen people of old, the people of Israel. In fact, one could say that the crisis which produced the Gospel of Matthew could be called 'an identity crisis'.

It is easy enough for us, today, to lose sight of just how much it would have cost the earliest Christians — mostly Jewish people — to leave their traditional faith and practice to enter a Christian community, such as the one which eventually produced the Gospel of Matthew. This was a most difficult journey for believing Jews to make, even though they may have come to believe that Jesus Christ was the Messiah. Their faith in Jesus of

Nazareth as the Christ, the Son of the living God (see 16:16) was causing them great suffering, as their long-time friends from the synagogue in the town could no longer abide the presence of these renegades in their community. In fact, we know that their old friends now prayed every morning:

> 'For apostates may there be no hope and may the Nazarenes and the heretics suddenly perish' (Twelfth Blessing of the synagogue prayer, the *Shemoneh Esreh*)

To be thrown out of the synagogue meant that almost every aspect of their day-to-day life was changed. They were snubbed by their former friends from 'the synagogue across the road'; they could no longer marry their sons and daughters within a community whose faith they shared and whose way of life they had always respected and also attempted to live. In a non-Jewish city (and Syrian Antioch looks like a good place for the birth of Matthew's Gospel), they were not even able to go into the confusion of the market place and buy their food from places where they had always been welcome, and where they knew it had been prepared in the time-honoured and sacred ways.

Although these practical difficulties were many, they would have laboured under an even greater problem. They were now separated from what was the heart of the life of a good Jew in the time when Matthew was writing his Gospel. They were excluded from the synagogue celebration of the Torah and its authoritative transmission by the Rabbi, the teacher, the authentic interpreter of the greatest of all teachers: Moses.

Cut off from the world that they knew and loved so much, they had to find a new 'Teacher' and a new authority. If the synagogue 'over the road' possessed Moses' Law and its authentic interpreter in the Rabbi (see, for example, 19:7 and 22:24) to whom could this struggling Jewish Christian Church now turn? We have already seen that the last words of Matthew's Gospel tell us: the early Church is commanded to teach all nations to observe all the things that Jesus had taught them (see 28:20). The Gospel of Matthew exists because this particular early Christian community took those words seriously and acted upon them.

Conclusion

Matthew has told his story of Jesus to a community which has been forcibly separated from Judaism, and which probably has many members longing for the old and trusted ways. He was very aware of the fragility of his own community, yet certain in his faith that God had broken into human history irrevocably in the birth, life, death and resurrection of Jesus. To bridge the gap between the old and the new, Matthew draws out of his story his central theme: during his life Jesus lived and asked for the perfection of the old ways, and then, through his death and resurrection the turning point of the ages came to pass.

Matthew tells his largely Jewish community that despite the hostility and the ridicule of the 'synagogue over the road' they have lost nothing. God's ways in the world have now been fulfilled, as the Old Testament has led to and been perfected in Jesus. The old ways are now perfected further in the universal presence of Jesus, through his Church, to the whole world. For Matthew, the true Israel is not to be found in the post-War synagogue stoutly defending its traditions to maintain its identity, but in the Christian community, now irrevocably committed to the Gentile mission.

Many of the Jewish people in Matthew's community were wondering if perhaps they had lost their way by becoming Christians, but Matthew's message dispels that doubt. He builds a bridge between the Old and the New, and that bridge is the person of Jesus. The puzzled members of Matthew's Church are told that they now belong to the new and perfect Israel, which has been given its new and perfect law by a new Moses on a new Sinai (see Mt 5:1-48).

Matthew never destroys the old; he has a deep respect for 2,000 years of sacred history. In fact, he rewrites Mark 2:22 which spoke of the uselessness of the 'old' wineskins, to show the permanent value of the 'old', side by side with the 'new':

> 'Neither is new wine put into old wineskins; if it is the skins burst, and the wine is spilled, and the skins are destroyed; but new wine is put into fresh wineskins, and so *both are preserved*' (Mt 9:17).

As he leads a traditional Jewish Christian community into the challenge of the Gentile mission he looks back to Jesus. He tells his story so that the community might see the perfection of the old, through the death and resurrection of Jesus, in the newness which they are living.

The Christian Church can never evade the challenge of the risen Lord questioning us and leading us into our 'Gentile mission'. We too must face the strange new ways and cultures that surround us, teaching them all that Jesus has taught. In our situation Matthew's Gospel tells us that we must allow ourselves to be led into a future which only God can create. Jesus will be with us until the close of the age. We are called to leave the securities of old and safe ways, yet always respecting those ways. They came into existence as the fruit of accumulated wisdom and experience. They are not to be simply discounted, as an appreciation of them prepares us for the newness of God's strange plans. God does not come to us 'new' in every new situation; he is always among us in a 'history of salvation', however much the turns of this history may surprise us.

Little wonder that Matthew described himself — and consequently all dedicated Christians — in a tiny biographical insertion which both gives his secret away and challenges all who follow him as disciples of Jesus:

> 'Every scribe who becomes a disciple of the kingdom of heaven is like a householder who brings out of his treasure things both new and old' (13:52).

THE GOSPEL OF MATTHEW AND THE LECTIONARY

The biblical scholar would be better pleased if the Church followed the text of the Gospel of Matthew throughout the whole of Year A of the Lectionary. In this way the celebrating community would be led through a systematic reading of the Gospel of Matthew in one liturgical year. But such a choice is not possible, nor would it be a wise or helpful one.

The liturgy is not only a school in the Word of God. The Church must pay prior attention to major moments in God's saving interventions in the human story. To celebrate those moments the Gospel passage suited to the event commemorated will be used, irrespective of the Gospel in which it is found. Thus, there are special readings for Advent, Christmastide, Lent and Easter. That leaves the thirty-four Sundays of the Ordinary Time of the Year. Although occasionally major feasts intervene, it is over the Ordinary Sundays of the Year that close attention can be paid to the systematic reading of the Gospel of Matthew. The selection of passages and their arrangement throughout the year of Matthew has its own problems. There are only thirty-four Ordinary Sundays of the Year, and the Gospel of Matthew is the longest of the Four Gospels. It is impossible to read every word of this Gospel within the limitations of the Sunday Gospels.

But even though not every word of the Gospel is read publicly, and there are places where the biblical scholar feels disappointed that certain key passages have not been chosen for a public reading, the passages selected still allow the overall plot of the Gospel to emerge for the reader. As we are all sometimes unaware of the unfolding argument of the Gospel story, I will present the use which the Sunday liturgy of Year A makes of the Gospel of Matthew during the Ordinary Sundays of the Year.

The presentation which follows presupposes the immediately previous chapter, where I outlined the shape and message of the Gospel. Particularly important are the pages devoted to 'The Plot of Matthew's Gospel' (see above, pp. 29-45). I will now attempt to situate each of the Sunday Gospels within the unfolding drama of the six narrative units which combine to form the overall plot of the Gospel of Matthew. This should guide the reader to an understanding of the context of the Gospel readings from one week to the next.

1. The coming of the Messiah (1:1—4:11)

The major part of this section of the Gospel is read over the Christmas period. God's promise of the Messiah, through the annunciation to Joseph (1:18-25) is read on the *Fourth Sunday of Advent*. The report of the crucial event which gives rise to all that happens, the birth of Jesus (see Mt 2:1a), is used for the *Feast of the Epiphany* (Mt 2:1-12), and the response of Israel to the birth of a King (2:13-23) is the Gospel reading for the *Feast of the Holy Family.*

Events which may have occurred several years later are still part of this first major section. They may take place at a later date, but they only happen because the Messiah has come; Jesus has been born (2:1a). The appearance of John the Baptist (3:1-12) is read on the *First Sunday of Advent*, and the Ordinary Sundays of the Year begin from this point. Understandably, a year dedicated to the reading of the ministry of Jesus as it is reported in the Gospel of Matthew begins with the account of his baptism (*First Sunday:* 3:13-17). But in order to prolong the story of John the Baptist, the Johannine account of his ministry of witness to Jesus as the Lamb of God and the Son of God is introduced (*Second Sunday:* Jn 1:29-34).

2. The Messiah's ministry to Israel (4:12—11:1)

The liturgy reports the key event of this section of the Gospel: the beginning of Jesus' ministry in Galilee (*Third Sunday:* 4:12-23). His ministry is marked by his preaching, teaching and healing (see 4:23-25; 9:35; 11:1). But the Lectionary chooses to concentrate more on Jesus' teaching rather than his miraculous activity. The sermon on the mount is used at length. The beatitudes (*Fourth Sunday:* 5:1-12) and the parables which insist on the need for those 'blessed' to be salt of the earth and light of the world (*Fifth Sunday:* 5:13-16) are reported in full. The theme of the perfection of the Law through Jesus' authoritative teaching is begun on one Sunday (*Sixth Sunday:* 5:17-37), and brought to its culmination on another as Jesus commands that the quality of Christian love produce a perfection that equals the perfection of God (*Seventh Sunday:* 5:38-48).

Throughout Mt 8-9 a series of miracles is reported, broken only by material in which Jesus either calls or instructs his disciples. The Lectionary uses the call of Levi (*Tenth Sunday:* 9:9-13) to show that Jesus' ministry will soon be shared by those whom he calls to follow him. It is unfortunate that, through the omission of the section of Matthew's Gospel devoted to Jesus' miracles, the Lectionary has not been able to show that Jesus was Messiah in Israel in both word and deed.

The teaching of Jesus to the twelve disciples (see 10:1) about how they are to repeat his ministry now follows. Three Sundays are devoted to Jesus' mission sermon. As he closes his miraculous activity he points to the need for labourers in the harvest, and then draws his disciples aside to instruct them (*Eleventh Sunday:* 9:36-10:8). A part of the mission will be the angry rejection which the missionaries will encounter. Jesus' words on this are not in the Lectionary (10:16-25, 34-36). However, more importantly, his words on the trust and confidence that the overwhelming care which God has for his missionaries, have their place (*Twelfth Sunday:* 10:26-33). But God and Jesus, the sent one of the Father, must be loved beyond all things. Such love must be shown by the way the Christian community cares for its missionaries, and all the 'little ones' who need support. In them the Church finds both Jesus and his Father (*Thirteenth Sunday:* 10:37-42).

3. The crisis in the Messiah's ministry (11:2—16:12)

The question of John the Baptist, which serves as the key to this section of the Gospel: 'Are you the one who is to come, or have we got to wait for someone else?' (11:3), is not in the Lectionary. Nevertheless we do find the criterion for the failure of Israel to accept the revelation of God in Jesus, in Jesus' teaching on God's revelation to the simple. It is not the wise who discover the revelation of God; it is God who makes himself known to the genuinely open disciple prepared to learn from his Son (*Fourteenth Sunday:* 11:25-30).

The parable discourse of Mt 13 begins with the parable of the sower and its interpretation. Both are found in the Lectionary. This Gospel reading highlights the special privilege granted to the followers of Jesus, over against the former chosen people who see but do not see, hear but do not hear. They are now excluded from Jesus' direct teaching; they are unable to understand the mystery revealed by the hidden language of the parables (*Fifteenth Sunday:* 13:1-23). In the following Sunday Gospel the parable of the weeds in the midst of the wheat tells of the Church as a 'mixed bag'. The Church is not the 'perfect society'. The good and the evil must be allowed to grow and exist together until the end of time. It is God who will decide what endures and what will be destroyed (*Sixteenth Sunday:* 13:24-43). This calls for a description of the kingdom of heaven, found in a series of similitudes. The privileged disciple, called to life in this kingdom, is finally described as a scribe trained to draw out of his treasure things both new and old (*Seventeenth Sunday:* 13:44-52).

Yet, even the disciples, to whom the mystery of the kingdom is revealed, stand by unable to understand as Jesus feeds the five thousand. They are people of 'little faith', failing to see the abundant goodness of God in the actions of Jesus (*Eighteenth Sunday:* 14:13-21). He comes to them across the waters, the revelation of God on the depths of the ocean to a barque which is the Church, but they all fear, and Peter doubts (*Nineteenth Sunday:* 14:22-33). The disciples may no longer belong to the traditional people of God which is hardening its attitude towards Jesus, but they still have a lot to learn. Jesus turns away from his own people, somewhat reluctantly, to reward the exceptional faith of the Canaanite woman (*Twentieth Sunday:* 15:21-28). Jesus does not abandon Israel, but he is now increasingly focusing his attention upon his disciples. They are the nucleus of the new nation which will believe in him, and the Canaanite woman looks towards all the nations who will hear his teaching and be baptised in the name of the Father, the Son and the Holy Spirit (see 28:16-20).

4. The Messiah's journey to Jerusalem (16:13—20:34)

The narrative used in the following two Sundays of the year gives an answer to John the Baptist's question: 'Are you the one who is to come' (11:3). But it also carries a serious challenge. Jesus is the Christ, the Son of God, and Peter's faith will make him the teacher and authority in the community which professes that faith (*Twenty-First Sunday:* 16:13-20). However, it is not enough to see Jesus as the glorious fulfilment of Israel's messianic hopes. Jesus is on his way to a cross, and he calls his disciples to follow him along a way of suffering (*Twenty-Second Sunday:* 16:21-27).

Once it has been made clear to the reader of the Gospel of Matthew that Jesus is the Christ and that disciples must follow him into suffering, the discourse on Christian community life can follow. It occupies two Sunday Gospels. The forgiveness available in the Christian community must surpass all imaginable limitations (*Twenty-Third Sunday:* 18:15-20), and the forgiveness of God depends upon the quality of the forgiveness in the community itself (*Twenty-Fourth Sunday:* 18:21-35). All human standards seem to be put into question, as the parable of the workers in the vineyard tells of the absolute authority of God who makes first those who are last (*Twenty-Fifth Sunday:* 20:1-16).

5. The Messiah's death and resurrection (21:1—28:15)

The crucial event of this narrative unit is the cleansing of the Temple (21:1-17). Jesus' words and actions in the Temple create a crisis because they confront the inhabitants of Jerusalem with his person and authority. They precipitate his death, as Israel rejects its Messianic King.

The Liturgy does not report this event, but moves directly to three parables. In these parables Jesus systematically attacks the leaders of Israel. They have rejected the offer God has made them in his Son. The parable of the two sons points to a people which only serves God with its lips (*Twenty-Sixth Sunday:* 21:28-32), while the parable of the wicked vinedressers tells the story of the failure and violence of those to whom the Lord's vineyard has been entrusted. The kingdom of God will be taken away from them and given to a nation producing fruit (*Twenty-Seventh Sunday:* 21:33-43). The third parable, the parable of the marriage feast, attacks both the original invitees, who reject their privileged invitation, and the Church itself, the guest without the wedding garment, unable to accept the blessings offered (*Twenty-Eighth Sunday:* 22:1-14).

Such an attack leads to further controversy, as the Jewish leaders attempt to get the better of Jesus through discussion. The Pharisees ask Jesus about the payment of tribute to Caesar, to trick him into showing disloyalty to either Caesar or the traditions of Israel, but are caught at their own game (*Twenty-Ninth Sunday:* 22:15-21). They return to the fray as they test Jesus' knowledge and understanding of the Law. They ask about the greatest commandment, only to be reduced to silence by a response they cannot deny (*Thirtieth Sunday:* 22:34-40). These controversies lead to Jesus' attack on the Scribes and the Pharisees, whom he accuses of hypocrisy and ambition. The Christian community is told that it has only one Master and Father, God in heaven, and only one Teacher, the Christ (*Thirty-First Sunday:* 23:1-12).

Jesus' final discourse is an instruction to his disciples, exhorting them to produce works of righteousness during the period of his absence. The Lectionary chooses two famous parables from this discourse. The parable of the wise and foolish bridesmaids instructs on the need to spend the waiting time in readiness for the bridegroom's arrival (*Thirty-Second Sunday:* 25:1-13). The parable of the talents makes the further point that one must not simply wait for his coming. There is a job to be done in the in-between time, so that the variety of gifts we have been given might bear fruit (*Thirty-Third Sunday:* 25:14-30).

The final Sunday of the year celebrates the universal kingship of Jesus Christ and one of the most singular elements in the Gospel of Matthew appears in the Liturgy for this day. Jesus will return as king and final judge in his glory. The judgment following his arrival obviously hangs upon how each 'sheep' or 'goat' has responded to Jesus himself. But, surprisingly, the yardstick is not the quality of prayer or the depth of union between the Christian and the Lord. Judgment will be exercised in terms of how we have treated the very least of those who belong to the household of God. We will not be judged by Jesus, the universal King. We will judge ourselves in our acceptance or refusal of the needy people around us (*Christ the King:* 25:31-46).

Having spoken to his disciples about their way of life when he will be separated from them, Jesus reminds them of his oncoming death and resurrection: 'Jesus had now finished all he wanted to say, and he told his disciples, "It will be Passover, as you know, in two days' time, and the Son of Man will be handed over to be crucified"' (26:1-2).

Conclusion

These pages on the use of the Gospel of Matthew in the Lectionary have not been written to provide a commentary on the individual passages for each Sunday. The commentaries which follow have that aim. I have attempted to trace the plot of the Matthean narrative, in order to present a picture, a bird's-eye-view, of the overall direction which this year's Lectionary takes.

As we read and listen to the Lectionary we should always be aware that this is the year of Matthew. Even though the words of the risen Jesus can come only at the end of the story, at the heart of the Gospel of Matthew lies the belief that the risen Jesus has been given all authority in heaven and on earth. We are sent to make disciples of all nations, teaching the things which he teaches us. This is a serious responsibility, but he is with us till the end of time (see 28:16-20).

Aware of his presence and open to his teaching we praise Jesus as our Lord and Christ as we respond to his Word with the joyful liturgical proclamation which I have taken for the title of this book: *The Gospel of the Lord!*

THE SEASON OF ADVENT

FIRST SUNDAY OF ADVENT

Matthew 24:37-44

Stay awake!

As we look forward to the feast of the Incarnation at Christmas, the first coming of Jesus, we are reminded of our place in history: after the Incarnation, waiting for the second coming. Advent is a season of the liturgical year which highlights the truth that the Christian life is lived between two special moments: God's gift of his Son which took place at a given time and in a given place, and his final coming to bring his creation to its perfect conclusion, at a time and in a way which are beyond our control or understanding.

The Gospel readings for this liturgical year begin with a reading drawn from the final days of Jesus' ministry, as they are recorded in the Gospel of Matthew. The readings for this year are dominated by the Gospel of Matthew. But, as the year begins, the Church chooses a reading which reminds us, not of the beginnings of Jesus' story, but of the end. Jesus points out that there is a close parallel between the decisive inbreak of God into the world at the end of time, 'when the Son of Man comes' (Mt 24:37) and the great flood story recorded in Genesis (Gen 6-8). The ordinary things in life went on. No attention was paid to the threatening presence of God's intervention which would make a judgment on the way such ordinary things were being done.

So will it also be in the day of the final coming of the Son of Man. The ordinary things in life will still be going on: people will be given and taken in marriage, they will continue to work in the fields or at the grindstone (v. 38).

The final coming of the Son of Man will make judgment upon these events: one will be saved and another lost (v. 41). It is not as if life is ever suspended. We are called to go on doing what we are best able to do in this world. However, it is the way in which we do these things that matters.

We are living the 'in between time'. As a Christian and a Eucharistic people, we have learnt from the life and teaching of Jesus that there is a quality of life asked from us which can transform the ordinary into the extraordinary, where everything shows forth God's love for us and our love for God. One day we will be judged according to our response to that knowledge.

When that day will be is beyond our knowledge and understanding. Indeed, it is a mystery beyond all understanding. Immediately before today's Gospel Jesus has said to his disciples: 'But of that day and hour no one knows, not even the angels of heaven, nor the Son, but the Father only' (v. 36).

Yet, as we look forward this Advent to the celebration of the first coming of the Son of Man, our Gospel reading summons us to recall the quality of life required from us, in expectation of the second and final coming of Jesus. We can be tempted to fall into a sleepy disrespect for all that is most important to our Christian lives. Indeed, we live in a modern world where those of us who attempt to live Christian values are regarded as quaint and outmoded. This can be difficult. Thus, as we begin Advent, Jesus calls to us: 'Stay awake!' There is much to be gained, both in this world and in the next, by a loving response to the ways of God, made known to us in the life and teaching of Jesus.

SECOND SUNDAY IN ADVENT

Matthew 3:1-12

The Kingdom of Heaven is at hand

At the beginning of the public ministry of Jesus, John the Baptist introduces Jesus, proclaiming the coming of the kingdom (Mt 3:2) in exactly the words which Jesus himself will later use: 'Repent, for the kingdom of heaven is at hand' (see 4:17). This prophet, dressed like Elijah the first of the prophets, calls for repentance; a response to God's action by a change in heart and mind about what is most important, and a consequent change in life-style.

But the Baptist does not appear upon the scene proclaiming repentance upon his own authority. He makes this appeal under the authority of the Word of God. Already the Prophet Isaiah had spoken of his voice, 'crying in the wilderness' (v. 3). Fulfilling God's design, as indicated by the prophecy of Isaiah, the Baptist attacks the traditional ways to God, those represented by the major religious institutions of Israel: the Pharisees and the Sadducees (v. 7).

The Pharisees were the people of the book, who took the Law to synagogues wherever there were Jews. The Sadducees were the priestly cast, offering sacrifice at the one Temple in Jerusalem. Neither of these ways to God is satisfactory. Like all the prophets before him, John the Baptist attacks any pretence to be religious, using expressions which reflect the fierce righteousness of God's prophet and the insidious wickedness that false religious practice produces: 'Brood of vipers' (v. 8). The institutions of Israel are attacked because they are not bearing the fruit which a true relationship with God will always produce. They act on the belief that they have a special place in God's hierarchy because of their link with Abraham (vv. 8-9). Blood ties are not the basis of oneness with God. As the Gospel of Matthew will show, the inexhaustible creative power of God can turn stones into children and Gentiles into disciples. One of Matthew's major concerns is to send out the Christian Church to bring the good news to all nations (see 28:16-20).

Despite his exalted role as the fulfilment of the prophecy of Isaiah and the precursor of the Messiah, John the Baptist concludes his witness by humbly subordinating his work and his person to Jesus. There is a design of God, in which one event follows another, one great prophet leads to another. The baptism of John is only a material rite leading to repentance, while Jesus will plunge us into the fiery experience of God's Holy Spirit (vv. 11-12). The one who follows John is, strangely, the stronger of the two. Normally the Master leads and 'the one who follows' learns. Here the roles are reversed (v. 11). The one who is to come is the Master, whose sandals the slave is not even worthy to carry.

The Church's use of John the Baptist over the Advent Season invites us to join John's audience in these days of preparation. The kingdom of heaven is at hand, and the one who is able to separate the wheat from the chaff is coming. In this 'in between time' we know and experience that we are already gifted with the presence of Christ among us, but does that influence our lives in any real and effective way? We too are waiting for the Christ who is still to come. What will be our response at his coming, both at Christmas and at the end of time?

THIRD SUNDAY OF ADVENT

Matthew 11:2-11

The least in the Kingdom of Heaven

Later in the ministry of Jesus John the Baptist wonders about Jesus of Nazareth. Lying in prison, he wonders if the man whose words and deeds are being reported to him is the one who is to come. If such is the case, then he can joyfully resign himself to whatever destiny may be ahead of him (Mt 11:2-3).

Jesus' response points to all he has done: the blind see, the lame walk, the deaf hear, the dead are raised to life and the Good News is proclaimed to the poor. All that had been foretold of the Messiah by the prophet Isaiah has been fulfilled superabundantly (see Is 35:5-6). There can be no doubt: Jesus is the 'one who is to come'. The first part of today's Gospel reading answers the question raised by John the Baptist.

But as the messengers depart, Jesus turns his attention away from a description of his own ministry as the fulfilment of a messianic prophecy from Isaiah. He speaks first of the virtue and courage of his forerunner, and then of the dignity and grandeur of all those who have been called to a privileged participation in the riches of God's kingdom. The Baptist is not just a prophet. He too fulfils messianic prophecies. This time the prophet cited by Jesus is Malachi (see Mal 3:1): the messenger sent before the messianic times. The reader is aware of this, as Jesus' ministry opened with the presentation of John the Baptist as the messianic forerunner.

But Jesus now adds further information on the greatness of the Baptist in God's story. Until the time of

Jesus, John the Baptist was the greatest of all human beings (v. 11). This is remarkable praise. As we look back over the great heroes of the story of Israel, the patriarchs, the judges, the kings, the wise men and women, the prophets, we are told that they pale into insignificance before the figure of John the Baptist. Whatever may have been their virtues and claims to greatness, John the Baptist has been a man committed to his call. He is no reed swaying in the breeze, or prince dressed in fine clothing. He is God's prophet, prepared to accept this task, cost him what it may (see vv. 7-10).

In this light, Jesus' closing words are all the more surprising. Despite the greatness of the figure of the Baptist, the disciple associated with Jesus in proclaiming the kingdom is superior. The Baptist fulfilled the Isaian prophecy of the forerunner. The 'least in the kingdom of heaven' is associated with Jesus in the greater mission of bringing hearing and sight, of giving power back to the legs of the lame. Above all, we are associated with Jesus in the proclamation of the Good News to the poor. We are not preparing the messianic era — we belong to it.

As the liturgy joins Jesus in speaking of the Baptist, we too can praise God for calling and gracing the great people from our sacred history. They have remained firm to their call, and 'made straight the paths of the Lord'. It is not only John the Baptist who has done this; we can all recall those special people of God in our lives. But what of our own dignity? Even the least of us is called to a greatness which surpasses that of the forerunner. This is 'good news' indeed, both encouragement and challenge.

FOURTH SUNDAY OF ADVENT

Matthew 1:18-24

The Emmanuel — God with us

Matthew's story of the birth of Jesus centres on the person of Joseph. Mary plays no active role in Matthew's story of the infancy of Jesus. Yet, like many of the women from Israel's sacred history, Mary has been strangely invaded by the power of God. The mystery is so great that even her betrothed cannot understand (see 1:19). In his puzzlement, the Lord calls Joseph to a remarkable act of faith and obedience.

Joseph is told of the origin of Mary's pregnancy through the message of the angel, coming to him in a dream. The child is 'in her by the Holy Spirit' (v. 20). However, what is more important for the Evangelist Matthew, as he begins his Gospel, is the proclamation of the future destiny of the son to be born. Along with Joseph, we learn that his name must be 'Jesus, because he is the one who will save his people from their sins' (v. 21).

The angel then announces that an ancient prophecy has been fulfilled: 'The virgin will conceive and give birth to a son and they will call him Emmanuel.' (v. 23). This prophecy was first made to one of the more sinful Kings of Israel, Ahaz. The prophet Isaiah asked him to abandon his own plans of war, and his plan to unite with one of Israel's neighbours in an attempt to overthrow the Egyptians (see Is 7:14). Isaiah asked that he trust more deeply in the goodness and power of YHWH. Ahaz disobeyed and was destroyed. Joseph, in wordless response to the word of God communicated by an angel, rose and 'took his wife to his home'. A total and unquestioning acceptance of the word of God is Joseph's first action in Matthew's infancy story.

But Matthew does not only report the fulfilment of the prophecy of Isaiah. He adds an explanation of what the word 'Emmanuel' means. Jesus' story begins with an indication that he will be the promised Emmanuel, which means 'God with us' (v. 23). As the Gospel of Matthew ends, the risen Jesus will announce to his infant Church: 'I am with you always, to the close of the age' (28:20).

Two things are happening in this story. On the one hand, God is now among us. By means of his messenger a child to be born of the Holy Spirit is announced. His word, originally proclaimed by a Prophet of YHWH is now being fulfilled. God is at the centre of the action, but we are learning how we should respond to God's interventions as Joseph, without argument or question, simply does what is asked of him.

Christmas brings us our Emmanuel. The celebration of Christmas reminds us that in the Incarnation God has become part of the human story. But Christmas also asks us to examine the quality of our response to the presence of the divine among us. Joseph leads the way and shows us the quality of trust and commitment to the coming of God, which should mark the lives of those blessed with the presence of Jesus, with them until the close of the age. As each Christmas comes and goes, the Church continues to proclaim that in Jesus, God is with us, and that Jesus will be with us until the end of time. May our joy and celebration be highlighted by deep trust in a God who so loved us that he gave his only Son (see Jn 3:16).

THE SEASON OF CHRISTMAS

CHRISTMAS NIGHT

Luke 2:1-14

A saviour has been born to you

We have been reading the Gospel of Matthew throughout Advent. The Church will use that Gospel for throughout this liturgical year, but because of the importance of Christmas, the Church turns to the Gospel of Luke for the celebration of Christmas night. It does this because of Luke's memorable story of Jesus' birth.

The Gospel of Luke deliberately links even the most sublime moments in God's dealings with the human story to events from that story. Luke's account of the birth of Jesus, the moment when the Son of God enters our story, opens with a series of names and places. Jesus did not simply come among us; he came into the world at a given place in a given time.

The names of the people involved begin with the greatest of human figures: Caesar Augustus, issuing a decree for a census of *the whole world*. His delegate, the slightly lesser Quirinius, looks to the area of *Syria*. Two simple people, Joseph and Mary, set out for *Bethlehem*, an insignificant town in Palestine. At Bethlehem they find that the usual resting places for travellers are full.

They began a journey from Nazareth which led them to Bethlehem. But there is no place for Jesus in the usual resting houses. Jesus is born on a journey, for a journey, and he will later call others to follow him. At birth he is wrapped, as a king, in swaddling cloths (see Wis 7:4-5), laid in a manger so that the prophecy of Isaiah might be reversed: 'The ox knows its owner and the ass its master's manger, Israel knows nothing, my people understands nothing' (Is 1:2-3).

The children of Israel summoned to the manger are not the high and the mighty. Shepherds are called from their flocks with the words: 'Today in the town of David a saviour has been born to you; he is Christ the Lord' (Lk 2:11). They are given the sign of the king in swaddling cloths and the manger at which Israel will be nourished. As they respond to the Word of God angels announce the glory of God and the wonders of his blessings upon all who are open to his goodness.

This famous Christmas story stands at the heart of much of our understanding of God's becoming man and dwelling among us. However, as the reading hints, there is more to it than the scene of a child in a stable. Luke's story of the birth of Jesus tells of a reversal of the value systems of the world. It opens with a list of people whom the world would regard the greatest (Caesar Augustus) to the less great (Quirinius) to the unimportant (Joseph and Mary). It closes with a song praising God who has given us a saviour in the newly born son of a humble woman, and who calls shepherds from their fields to be the first to acknowledge their Christ and Lord.

Christmas time in Australia can sometimes lead to a search for the gift with the correct label. But, more significantly, it is a time when we are able to stop and re-assess our values. The liturgy tonight announces that a people who walked in darkness has seen a great light (Is 9:1). May this night be filled with the light of *love given* and *love received*, reflecting in our lives the love of our God who has entered our story in the birth of his Son, Jesus Christ.

CHRISTMAS DAY*

John 1:1-18

The Word was made flesh

Stories surrounding Jesus' birth were developed in the preaching of the early Church to capture the wonder of God's action in sending his only Son to be our Saviour. We have been reading some of these stories, taken from the Gospels of Matthew and Luke during Advent and on Christmas night. In the final liturgy for the celebration of Christmas day, the Prologue to the Gospel of John is used by the Church to summarise the significance of the events celebrated at Christmas.

The Prologue has always been rightly remembered for its famous words 'the Word became flesh and dwelt among us' (Jn 1:14). However, this Gospel reading tells us more about the Incarnation than the fact of the Word's becoming flesh and dwelling among us. Several times through the hymn the author repeats a message which is basic to Christianity. The Word exists from all time (v. 1), well before the Baptist, his God-sent witness (vv. 6-8, 15), in a union with God so close that what God is, the Word also is (v. 2). But to speak a 'Word' means to communicate a message. God speaks, and the Word who is one with God dwells among us (v. 14). This Word provides the only place among us where we can find God. No one has ever seen God, but Jesus Christ, the Word of God, makes God known to us (v. 18).

* For the Gospel reading of the Christmas Dawn Mass (Lk 2:15-20), see the reflection of the Feast of Mary, the Mother of God. John 1:1-18 is also the Gospel reading for the Second Sunday of Christmas, a Sunday liturgy generally absorbed by the Feasts of either the Holy Family or Mary, the Mother of God.

The Word shines in our darkness (v. 5); the Word comes unto his own (v. 11); the Word is the fulness of a gift which is the Truth (v. 17). How we respond to the gift of the Word is up to us. God will not force his truth upon us. He may have come to his own people, but they did not receive him (v. 11). He shines in the darkness, but the darkness still attempts to overcome the Word (v. 5). Where do we stand? The Gospel promises that all those who accept the Word spoken by God in the person of Jesus Christ become children of God (v. 13). We are not born of any human means, but through the gift of God himself.

This is certainly poetry, but (like all great poetry) is it not also our experience? We do not *earn* the gift of faith through our own good works or intelligence. Through all sorts of coincidences — birth, friends, religious experience, a word passed on in time of need — we are *drawn* to the Word who became flesh. It is important for us to recognise the gift which is ours, and thus to treat it as that which is most precious.

Unlike many gifts, the gift of the Word will give life and light if we respond to its challenge. The light still shines in our darkness, but we remain free, able to choose between light or darkness in all the events of our every day lives. Our freedom to say yes or no to a never-failing light summoning us to life, is remarkable evidence of God's love for us. Whilst freedom is the greatest feature of the human being, nowhere do we exercise it more crucially than in our acceptance or refusal of the Word who became flesh, and who dwells among us.

THE HOLY FAMILY

Matthew 2:13-15. 19-23

The man from Nazareth

Repeatedly, the angels of the Lord lead Joseph into strange behaviour. He is asked to take to himself a young woman who is already with child by the Holy Spirit — whatever that might have meant to him (Mt 1:18-25)! He is further asked to flee his homeland to set out for Egypt (2:13-15). In our own times this may not seem such an ordeal but for the first century Jew, a journey to Egypt would have been a traumatic experience. Joseph does so on the basis of a command from an angel of the Lord (2:13). The ways of God must have seemed strange to this 'just man' but through his obedience the Christ is born to the world.

Today's Gospel tells us of the journey of Joseph, Mary and their child back from Egypt to the Promised Land. I have chosen my words carefully: 'Egypt to the Promised Land'. This is not just a memory of something that happened in the story of the infant Jesus. The backdrop to this story is another great moment in God's saving plan. Jesus is repeating the experience of Moses. Indeed, the flight into Egypt had already been occasioned by an event which parallelled the experience of Moses. At Moses' birth many innocent Hebrew baby boys were slain (see Ex 1:15-2:10). So also with the birth of Jesus, where the innocents of Bethlehem are slain by the soldiers of Herod (Mt 2:16-18).

After the death of Herod, as Moses had come from Egypt, so Jesus, the man who surpasses all that Moses had been and done, comes out of Egypt. The words of

Hosea, originally recalling the experience of the Exodus, now apply to Jesus: 'I called my son out of Egypt' (Hos 11:1).

Joseph responds happily to a further divine intervention into his life and leads his family back to their own land . . . but again he is 'warned in a dream' (Mt 2:19). There can be no returning to his home in Bethlehem.

Along with Joseph and Mary, Jesus is to be a wanderer, unwanted and persecuted by the powers in the land, but responding trustingly and unfailingly to the ways of God. Indeed, the experiences of the adult Christ are already foreshadowed in his infancy. As was the case with the flight into Egypt, his further flight into Nazareth may have been difficult, but it fulfilled the promises of God, made through the prophets: 'He will be called a Nazarene' (v. 23).

Throughout the infancy story of Jesus there have been repeated references to the fulfilment of the sayings of one or other of the prophets. This final saying, 'He will be called a Nazarene', cannot be found in any specific prophet. Matthew does not link the words with 'a prophet', but claims that it fulfils all that 'the prophets' had said. There is a long line of many prophets, indeed the whole prophetic presence of the word of God in the story of Israel, behind this final word on Jesus, the man from Nazareth.

Throughout his life Jesus will be known as Jesus of Nazareth. At his death, his final act of obedience, a sign will be placed on the Cross: Jesus of Nazareth, the King of the Jews (Mt 27:37). In this way the words spoken through the prophets are fulfilled. To be family, Joseph, Mary and Jesus had to accept so much that was difficult, from flight to crucifixion. It is this all-too-common aspect of suffering in our family life that we also must be prepared to accept in some way as part of God's presence in our lives.

MARY, MOTHER OF GOD

Luke 2:16-21

Treasuring in the heart

The Gospel today is devoted largely to the story of the shepherds' discovery of a newly born child, and his being named 'Jesus'. Even though not reported in the reading for the liturgy, we are aware that the shepherds have responded to the command of an angel to visit a newly born King. They set out to find the King, and find 'Mary and Joseph and the babe lying in the manger' (Lk 2:16).

It would appear that the story of the birth of Jesus and the shepherds' proclamation that he is a King, born in a manger, was about Jesus. Yet the Church has used it to celebrate the feast of Mary as the Mother of God because towards the end of the story it is Mary's response to Jesus' birth which is important for the story-teller.

There are three possible reactions to the wonders accompanying the birth of Mary's child. We read of 'everyone who heard it' that they are astonished at what the shepherds have had to say. However, there is no indication that their 'hearing' leads to faith. Nor do they make any attempt to 'see' the newly born child. All they do is wonder (v. 18).

The shepherds, on the other hand, respond to the command of the angels that they go and find this child, wrapped in swaddling cloths and lying in a manger (vv. 7, 12, 16). The biblical traditions record that Kings are to be wrapped in the tight bands, swaddling cloths, which ensure healthy limbs (see Wis 7:4-5). The child is laid in a manger, the source of all future nourishment for those who would care to look to him in faith, hope and love (see Is 1:2-3). After these events the shepherds go back to their fields (v. 20). They are never heard of again. No shepherds stand by when Jesus of Nazareth begins his public ministry, able to remember the wonders of his birth.

However, set between 'those who heard' and simply wonder, and the shepherds who disappear from the story is a woman who is present during the life and death of Jesus, and who is still present in the life of the Church: Mary. We are told that 'she treasured all these things and pondered them in her heart' (v. 19).

Often throughout the Bible, women and men receive revelations from God which are beyond their ken. The person of true faith, unable to understand the mysteriousness of God's ways, treasures and dwells upon them with ultimate trust in God, waiting to be led where God wills. So it is with Mary. Though unable to understand fully what has happened to her, she has said 'yes', and from then on laid herself open to the plan of God.

Mary is presented in the Gospel of Luke as the Mother of Jesus, the one who bears the Son of God. Her acceptance of God's ways enabled her to play this role. Mary, however does not only bear the Son of God in her body. Her faithful acceptance of God's will shows her as a person who also bears him in her heart and soul. Thus, Mary is not the only one who 'bears the Son of God'. As Christian believers and as a Christian Church we learn to wait *patiently and trustingly* in the midst of misunderstanding so that we too may bring Jesus Christ into our world. Today's Gospel presents Mary as Mother, not only of the Son of God, but also of a humble, trusting Church.

EPIPHANY

Matthew 2:1-12

A child reveals God to the world

Christian tradition has long associated the visit of the three Magi to the infant Jesus with the celebration of God's making his Son known to the whole world. Indeed, this is a proper understanding of the figures of the Magi in the Gospel of Matthew. Today's celebration of the Feast of the Epiphany demands a reading of, and a reflection upon, the story of the Magi. But the most important element in this Gospel passage are the actors in the story, especially the Magi, and not the star of Bethlehem.

On the one hand, we have the story of some 'wise men' who come from the east. They were not born and bred within the traditions and beliefs of Israel. They do not form part of the 'chosen people', but they come to render homage to a new-born King. Following the indications of a star, which they read as the sign marking the birth of a King, they come to the right place: Jerusalem (Mt 2:1-2). In the Holy City, and in the Holy Scriptures of the Chosen People the truth will be found. Indeed, they are told the correct answer: the Scriptures have foretold that the Messiah will be born in Bethlehem (vv. 4-6).

Filled with delight as they follow the star, the wise men find the child in Bethlehem, fall to their knees and offer their gifts of gold, frankincense and myrrh — symbols of Jesus' being born to be a king — unto death (vv. vv. 10-11). Finally, they humbly and obediently respond to the Lord's warning about Herod which they receive in a dream, and 'returned to their own country by a different way' (v. 12). They might not belong to a people 'chosen' by history or culture, but they were 'chosen' by God from the Gentile world, and they came in faith and love.

This story of a joyful and positive response from the wise men is matched by the opposite reaction from those who should have known better. The wise men come to Jerusalem, the sacred city of God, and ask for further knowledge about the new-born King (vv. 1-2). Indeed, the chief priests and the scribes are able to provide the information: Bethlehem (vv. 4-6)! They know the answers from their sacred tradition, but they do not have the openness to the revelation of God present in this child born to be king. Herod and the whole of Jerusalem are perturbed (v. 3). This consternation will eventually lead to the slaying of the Innocents (vv. 16-18). There are dark hints of what might soon happen as Herod interrogates the Magi 'privately', so that he too may offer homage (vv. 7-8)!

While today the Church proclaims the revelation of God to the whole world — in the figures of the wise men from the east — it also warns all who have been blessed with the 'knowledge' of the truth. The Magi have no special privileges; they simply respond to the sign which comes from God. The Chosen People in their Holy City with their Holy Scriptures are threatened when their 'religion' is disturbed by Jesus. We 'chosen ones', with our Catholic history and culture, can also miss the wonder of God's presence in our lives, because it challenges our own tidy schemes too radically. The life and teaching of Jesus will always threaten our comfort, and call us to great love. It is one thing to say that we have our answers in the person and teaching of Jesus; it is another to live lives which show such answers to be true.

THE BAPTISM OF THE LORD

Matthew 3:13-17

All that righteousness demands

In the Infancy Story (Mt 1-2), God made his plans known to women and men. Jesus has been born to Mary, and is cared for by Joseph, but he never did or said anything. Only with his Baptism at the Jordan does Jesus actively enter the story. Jesus came from Galilee to the Jordan to be baptised by John (Mt 3:13). There is no hesitation here. Decisions have been made by Jesus to begin his ministry, and so he travels the length of Israel to come to the Jordan to be baptised by John the Baptist.

However, the Baptist is unhappy that Jesus should submit himself to such a process. Recognising his subordinate place in God's plans, he suggests that Jesus should be baptising him (v. 14). But there is something deeper happening in this little drama. John the Baptist is certainly only a forerunner, a part of the Old Testament, preparing the way for God's new messianic age which will begin with Jesus of Nazareth. Now that Jesus is in the story, is it not fitting that the Baptist should stand aside?

No, because, there is a larger plan of God behind Jesus' story. Jesus' ministry must be lived out within Israel, and in accordance with all righeousness (v. 15). Jesus did not come to do away with the Law and the Prophets. He came to bring them to perfection (see 5:17-18). It is for this reason that Jesus tells John the Baptist that, 'for the time being' things must go along their established course. There will be a time in the future when things will change, when God's ways with the world will be larger than the fulfilment of the Jewish law and the hopes of the Jewish prophets.

God's design is, however, that Jesus perfect all that was best in Israel. He will be slain for such a lifestyle, but that will open a new era in God's saving presence to the world. The Baptist, as always open to the ways of God, consents to the word of Jesus and accepts the plan of God (v. 15).

Once both Jesus and John the Baptist have shown a preparedness to accept God's design, then God makes it known that he is present in the man Jesus. In the ancient world, where God was understood as above the heavens and the human drama was being acted out 'below', the tearing open of the heavens indicated that heaven and earth were about to meet. Gently as a dove, the Spirit of God descends upon Jesus (v. 16). A voice from heaven proclaims: 'This my beloved Son, with whom I am well pleased' (v. 17). God's pleasure comes from Jesus' acceptance of his plans. How easy it would have been to accept the Baptist's recognition, to take over the dominant role. But he did not, because Jesus must follow the plan of God. He must 'do all that righteousness demands' (v. 15). Jesus has already pleased God in his first public appearance. His story will go on pleasing God.

As we move from the joyful celebration of the Christmas Season, the Church leads us into the Ordinary Sundays of the Year. Jesus' response to the Baptist and God's response to his openness to his plan instruct us as we are about to face the blessing and the problems, the joys and the pains, the hard work and the leisure, of the year that lies ahead. God's pleasure will be with us if we, like Jesus, do our best ask what God might want of us. We too are asked to 'do all that righteousness demands'.

THE SEASON OF LENT

FIRST SUNDAY OF LENT

Matthew 4:1-11

The testing of God's Son

Matthew's Baptism of Jesus closes with the words of a voice from heaven: 'This is my beloved Son, with whom I am well pleased' (Mt 3:17). Today's Gospel follows immediately. The claims of the voice from heaven, that Jesus is God's Son, are tested by the tempter through the repetition of the expression: 'If you are the Son of God' (see vv. 3, 6). Background to the discussion is the teaching of the Book of Deuteronomy, reflecting an earlier experience in the desert. When Israel was a wandering people, the Israelites were instructed on all that they must do to be God's children (see Deut 6 and 8).

The tempter uses words taken from the scriptures of the Book of Deuteronomy to test Jesus. If he really is God's Son, then he should use this privilege for his own advantage. In his baptism he surrendered himself to God, and that is now under threat. The Baptist had attempted to avoid the baptism, but Jesus had insisted: 'It is fitting that we should, in this way, do all that righteousness demands' (3:15).

The first sign of Jesus' sonship would be his ability to make food from stones to feed the multitudes (Mt 4:3. See Deut 6:10-11; 8:3). This may also be a temptation to be a political messiah, but Jesus' reply — also quoting Deuteronomy (Deut 6:3) — tells of a trustful waiting for God's help. It is God's word which creates and sustains humankind in all its needs: 'Man does not live on bread alone but on every word that comes from the mouth of God (Mt 4:4. See Deut 8:3).

The devil seizes on Jesus' trust in God and challenges him to a presumptuous demonstration of such trust. The Son of God will be supported and cared for by the angels of God (see Ps 91:11-12). But again Jesus fights this false manipulation of the Scriptures with a total openness to the word of God. True trust includes an obedience which allows God to be God. There must be no forcing of God's hand . . . as there can be no forcing of God's scriptures (4:7).

The final temptation reveals the horror of the contest. The outward appearance of the encounter between Jesus and Satan tests Jesus' sonship. But more than that: it is a struggle between God and Satan. Where will Jesus place his allegiance? The whole world is at stake, as the question is: who is truly God? Will Jesus follow Israel's history of idolatry? For the true Son of God further debate is impossible. There is only one God and 'You must worship the Lord your God and serve him alone' (4:23. See Deut 6:13). Showing the Son's unshaken union with his Father, Satan is sent packing: 'Be off, Satan!'.

The all-too-common Christian search for the wonders which can accompany true faith is severely questioned in today's Gospel. Miracle workers, prophets and teachers abound. In a world where there is so much insecurity on the one hand, and so many modern wonders on the other, none of which finally resolve our many difficulties, many of us flock to find the sensational, the wonder which will finally prove that I am right in my beliefs. Our being children of God is not a matter of miracles, but of understanding God's will through openness to his word and carrying it out in love, trust and obedience.

SECOND SUNDAY OF LENT

Matthew 17:1-9

No place to pitch a tent

Throughout the latter part of the Gospel of Matthew, Jesus begins to warn his disciples that he is going up to Jerusalem, and there he must suffer many things, be killed, and rise again (see Mt 16:13-28; 17:22-23; 20:17-19). But as Jesus moves towards his death, the journey to Jerusalem and death is strangely interrupted by an unexpected moment of glory.

Jesus takes three disciples to the top of a mountain (Mt 17:1). Because of Israel's experience of Sinai, mountains are places where God makes himself known. Before their eyes Jesus is transfigured. The description of his transfigured form comes from the language which Jewish thinkers were using to speak of the appearance of the Messiah at the end of time (v. 2). The final appearance of the Messiah in glory is partially experienced on the mountain. In the middle of a journey towards suffering, Jesus appears before three of his disciples as the glorious Messiah.

But the disciples witness not only the transfigured Jesus. 'Suddenly' Moses and Elijah are there, in conversation with him (v. 3). The Law, the Prophets and Jesus are one. The disciples find themselves at the crossroads of God's salvation history. The Law established a covenant with a chosen people. The prophets performed the task of continually reminding the people of the covenant and of chastising them in their unfaithfulness. Both the Law and the prophets looked forward to God's final intervention into the human story. The disciples are witnesses to that intervention.

However, the disciples have a problem. They would like to stop God's history. Peter suggests that tents be set up so that this moment of truth can be held, a static vision for all to behold (v. 4). He is happy to settle for that particular truth-filled moment. This cannot be. While he is still making this suggestion a voice from the clouds affirms that Jesus is the Son of God. Indeed, he is the beloved Son of God. This means that the way he responds to God makes him special. He enjoys God's favour, but if the disciples are to fully understand all that is happening in and through Jesus they must listen to his voice (v. 5).

The excitement of being with Moses, Elijah and the glorious Messiah turns into fear for the disciples. The glory disappears. A person who is now 'only Jesus' touches them, encourages them, and together they descend the mountain. On the way down the mountain he hints that the glory they have known briefly will only be his through the experience of suffering and death: 'risen from the dead'.

As Lent begins, the Church has us proclaim the story of the transfiguration to teach us that there is no place for the disciple of Jesus to pitch a tent, to dwell on the moments of success and truth which occasionally come our way. We too are privileged to stand within God's salvation history: between the givenness of the Law, the prophets and the life, death and resurrection of Jesus. At times we are touched by hints of the glory which lies ahead, but to settle for 'the seeds of the promise' while still on the journey would be to miss the promise itself. The season of Lent instructs that we must follow a suffering Jesus along a way of the Cross to come with him to glory.

THIRD SUNDAY OF LENT

John 4:5-42

We have heard for ourselves

The encounter between Jesus and the Samaritan woman and the Samaritan villagers is a story of the possibility of a journey from no faith, to partial faith to full faith. After overcoming the original shock that a Jew would even speak to a Samaritan woman (Jn 4:9), she cannot grasp what Jesus is offering her. He tells her: 'Anyone who drinks *the water that I shall give* will never be thirsty again'. She can only think of ordinary water and ordinary thirst. She cannot accept his words: 'Give me some of that water that I may never get thirsty . . . *and have to come here again to draw water*' (vv. 13-15).

But Jesus, reaching outside Judaism into the missionary world for the first time in his story, takes her gently into something that she can understand: her marital situation (vv. 16-18). Now Jesus' words suggest to her that he is a prophet (v. 19). A discussion between a Jewish prophet and a Samaritan over the right place for worship leads Jesus to announce that there will no longer be a 'place'. True worship happens 'in spirit and truth' (vv. 20-24). She now suspects that he might even be the promised Messiah: 'Come and see a man who has told me everything I ever did; I wonder if he is the Christ?' (v. 29. See also vv. 25-26). She has gone beyond her first response to the promise of Jesus. Now she thinks that he might be the Messiah. We are soon to discover that he is more than the Messiah.

The Samaritan villagers are aroused by her curious story, go to the well to see Jesus and invite him to stay with them (v. 30). At first they believe in Jesus because of the woman's words (v. 39). After hearing him themselves, they come to believe in him because of his word. On the basis of the word of Jesus they arrive at an understanding that transcends all the woman had suggested. Jesus is not only a prophet and the Messiah; 'He really is the saviour of the world' (v. 42).

The story of the Samaritan woman and the Samaritan villagers teaches us of the possibilities of faith. The woman goes from no faith in Jesus, hoping that he will provide for her material needs (vv. 5-15), to a partial faith, suspecting that he might be her expected Messiah (vv. 16-19). The villagers finally come to see that he is the saviour of the world (vv. 39-42).

We too are capable of repeating the initial experience of the Samaritan woman. Often we simply do not hear the word of Jesus because we are too concerned with our own needs. Most of the time, however, we are happy to believe in Jesus. But if we reflect upon the quality of our faith we will see that, like the Samaritan woman again, we commit ourselves to faith in the Jesus of our expectations. As long as he is our prophet and the messiah we are waiting for, we are comfortable. Only occasionally we listen to the word of Jesus and risk everything in confessing that he is the saviour of the world.

Most of us live the major part of our lives perched somewhere between apostasy and sanctity. We do not have the courage to go one way or the other. We need not be discouraged by this. Today's Gospel asks us to recognise the limitations of our faith, and to see the possibilities of an unconditional commitment to the word of God, made known to us in Jesus.

FOURTH SUNDAY OF LENT

John 9:1-41

Blindness to sight — sight to blindness

The story of the man born blind but who is given sight is also the story of a group of people who move from sight to blindness. There was a man who had been born blind. The fact that he was 'born blind' means that he has never seen the light. Coming to sight will be his first encounter with the light (Jn 9:1-5). Through contact with Jesus, whose name is found in the very waters of the pool of Siloam, he regains his physical sight (vv. 6-7). That is only the beginning of a longer and more serious story of people who start by suspecting that Jesus might be a miracle worker, but who end by claiming that Jesus is a sinner.

After the brief account of the miracle, where the waters of the pool of Siloam are interpreted as the person of Jesus, 'the sent one' (v. 7), the man born blind is subjected to a series of interrogations. However, even though the man is being asked many questions, it is really Jesus who is being tried in his absence. Through one interrogation after another the cured man 'sees' more clearly who Jesus is. To his own friends he says: 'The man called Jesus' had worked the miracle (vv. 8-12), but at the end of his first interrogation by the Pharisees, he goes further: 'He is a prophet' (vv. 13-17).

Abandoned by his parents 'for fear of the Jews', he must undergo a further abusive interrogation, but he becomes bolder. He finally teaches his interrogators: 'If this man were not from God, he couldn't do a thing' (vv. 24-34). Jesus re-enters the story to find the one who has come very close to true belief, now cast out of the

Synagogue by the Pharisees (v. 34). He presents himself as the Son of Man whom the once blind man can now see and hear: 'The man said, "Lord, I believe", and worshipped him' (vv. 35-38). A journey into the fulness of sight has come to an end. A once blind man prepared to admit there were many things that he could not know or understand (see vv. 12, 25, 36) now sees.

But another journey has been taking place as the blind man came to full sight. At first the Pharisees accept the miracle, but are divided over its divine origins (v. 16). Then, in an attempt to show that there never was a miracle, they call for the evidence of the parents, but the parents will not be drawn into the argument, as they fear the Jews who will drive out of the Synagogue anyone who confesses that Jesus is the Christ (vv. 18-23). Foiled in this the Pharisees resort to abuse, giving total allegiance to Moses, regarding this man, whose origins they do not know, as a sinner (vv. 24-34). A journey away from sight has come to an end. Full of their knowledge and authority (see vv. 24, 29, 31), the custodians of the traditional faith have fallen into blindness.

It is Jesus' own words which conclude this dual journey: 'If you were blind, you would not be guilty, but since you say, "We see", your guilt remains'. The blind man was always prepared to say, 'I do not know', and to look towards Jesus, the Son of Man, as the giver of true light. The Pharisees were full of their own plans and knowledge, but this only led them on a journey into blindness. Lent is a time to examine where we have placed our hopes — in our own confident knowledge and self-trust, where God hardly has a place, or in a ready admission of our need for the good gifts God alone gives us.

FIFTH SUNDAY OF LENT

John 11:1-45

Death or glory?

On being told that the man whom he loved was ill, Jesus replied: 'This sickness will not end in death, but in God's glory, and through it the Son of God will be glorified' (Jn 11:4). The larger story of God stands behind both the initial delay, and the eventual decision that — despite the danger — Jesus will set out for Jerusalem. The story of the resurrection of Lazarus is also the story of the beginnings of Jesus' glorification. By means of the miracle of Lazarus the glory of God will shine forth in the crucified Messiah (see v. 4)

On Jesus' arrival, two sisters play important roles in the unfolding of the drama (vv. 19-20). Martha went to meet him, unhappy that he was not with them to prevent their tragedy. Jesus' promise to Martha that Lazarus will rise leads her to re-state Jewish hopes, that there will be a resurrection on the last day (vv. 25-27). Jesus has challenged her to go further than these limited hopes. There is no need to wait for the end of time for life; Jesus himself is the resurrection and the life (v. 25-26). There can be no death for those who believe in him. Despite her good will, she cannot accept Jesus' self-proclamation. She claims that she believes, but her confession: 'You are the Christ, the son of God, the one who is to come into the world' can be understood as a profound Jewish confession of faith in the expected Messiah (v. 27). Such faith is still not enough; it forms part of her culturally conditioned religious hopes and expectations.

Mary also expresses her sorrow at Jesus' late arrival (vv. 32-33), but she leads him into his frank expression of sorrow, affection and the crucial question: 'Where have you put him?' (vv. 33-34). While Martha's encounter led to *words* which proclaimed Jesus as the resurrection and the life, Mary's leads to *action* which proclaims the same truths (vv. 39-44).

The resurrection of Lazarus — still wearing the signs of death to which he will return — produces faith among many, but the story returns to where it began: the oncoming death of Jesus. Caiaphas informs the Pharisees: 'One man must die for the people' (v. 50). But the storyteller adds that the effects of this death will reach further: 'not for the nation only, but to gather together in unity the scattered children of God' (v. 52).

Jesus' life-giving presence is double edged. 'God so loved the world that he gave his only Son — not to judge the world — but to save the world'. This is the Jesus whose death and resurrection we are about to celebrate. True life cannot be had without death. There is no glory without death. Lazarus comes to life, as Jesus turns towards a death which will give eternal life. However, the life restored to Lazarus is temporary. This is indicated by the clothes of death he is still wearing as he comes forth from the tomb (v. 43-44). The life which the death of Jesus produces will last forever. This will be indicated at the resurrection of Jesus, where the clothes of death will be found carefully wrapped, and laid to one side (see Jn 20:6-7). The wonder of Lazarus' resurrection is simply that — wonder. The resurrection of Jesus brings eternal life.

PALM SUNDAY

Matthew 26:14—27:66

The turning point of the ages

The first words of Matthew's passion story betray one of his special concerns. While Mark begins with the plot to slay Jesus, Matthew tells his reader that all the teaching of Jesus is finished: 'Jesus had now finished all he wanted to say' (Mt 26:1). He then prophesies his own passion: 'It will be Passover, as you know, in two days' time, and the Son of Man will be handed over to be crucified' (v. 2).

All that is about to happen is not mere chance. Jesus himself tells the disciples, and the reader of Matthew's Gospel, that it is part of God's story. God is behind the passive verb 'will be handed over'. The passion is part of the fulfilment promised in 5:17: 'Do not imagine that I have come to abolish the Law or the Prophets. I have come not to abolish but to complete them'. In 26:1-2 God's program has been stated. We now go on to read how it happened.

Matthew, following a scheme already used in the Gospel of Mark, presents alternating scenes in which disciples fail, while Jesus commits himself both to them and to the ways of his Father. This can again be seen in the following scheme, where [A] indicates the theme of failure while [B] shows Jesus' betrayal and mounting violence.

[A] vv. 3-5: The plot against Jesus — *FAILURE*
[B] vv. 6-13: The anointing for death — *JESUS*
[A] vv. 14-16: Betrayal of Judas — *FAILURE*
[B] vv. 17-19: Preparation for the Passover — *JESUS*
[A] vv. 20-25: Prediction: the betrayal of Jesus — *FAILURE*

[B] vv. 26-29: The Supper — *JESUS & FAILING DISCIPLES*
[A] vv. 30-35: Prediction: Peter's denial — *FAILURE*
[B] vv. 36-46: Gethsemane — *JESUS*
[A] vv. 47-56: Jesus arrested and disciples flee — *FAILURE*
[B] vv. 57-68: The Jewish trial of Jesus — *JESUS*
[A] vv. 69-75: Peter denies Jesus — *FAILURE.*

Although Matthew is using a pattern to tell the story which he has taken from the Gospel of Mark, our Evangelist insinuates his own point of view. An example of this can be found in the way Matthew reports the last meal of Jesus with his disciples. Matthew intensifies the portrait of failing disciples. In the narrative before the meal (Mt 26:21-25) the Evangelist Matthew *heightens* the drama of Judas' betrayal. Mark has a general indication that 'one of you' (Mk 14:18), 'one of the twelve' would betray him (14:20). This indication is followed by the lament over 'that man by whom the Son of Man is betrayed' (14:21). Judas is never named, nor does he enter the story actively. The reader knows who is in question.

Matthew deliberately refashions Mark's version of the story and even the words of Jesus to stress Judas' failure. Jesus first indicates generally 'one of you is about to betray me' (Mt 26:21). He then shifts away from Mark's reference to one of the Twelve 'who is dipping into the same dish with me' (Mk 14:20) to state with specific reference to an action already completed before the eyes of all: 'Someone has dipped his hand into the dish with me' (Mt 26:23). After the lament over the betrayer, Matthew has Judas himself enter the story: 'Judas, who was to betray him, asked in his turn, "Not I, Rabbi, surely?" "They are your own words" answered Jesus' (26:25). In Matthew, little is left to the imagination. One of the Twelve, whose name was Judas, is the betrayer. Matthew sets the scene of a clearly defined and named disciple who has shared a sacred meal with Jesus. He can now tell the story of the supper itself.

A feature of the Matthean account of the meal which must be noticed. Only Matthew adds to Jesus' words over the cup: 'for the forgiveness of sins' (Mt 26:28). There is widespread agreement among scholars that Matthew has made explicit what was implicit in the other traditions: the new covenant presupposes the forgiveness of sins. All other words over the cup make reference to the covenant (see Mk 14:24; Lk 22:20; 1 Cor 11:25), but only Matthew has words on the lips of Jesus which speak of a covenant 'for the forgiveness of sins'.

Matthew's explicit reference to the blood of the covenant poured out for many *for the forgiveness of sins* (v. 28) reflects both the Matthean community's own liturgical practice, and the Evangelist's message that by sharing the one bread and drinking the one cup, the disciples share in the saving effects of Jesus' atoning sacrifice. However, what is Matthew's context here? Which disciples will share in the saving effects of Jesus' atoning sacrifice? The answer is clear: Jesus breaks his body and pours out his blood for the disciples mentioned both before and after the account of the meal itself. The forgiveness which is offered is certainly linked to the promise of the new covenant, but it is also linked to the sinfulness of the betrayers and deniers who are sharing the meal with Jesus himself.

Matthew's version of the account of the future denials of the disciples, which follows the meal, adds weight to this argument. Matthew again makes the disciples' failure more specific. Mark has Peter claim that he would never fail Jesus, 'even if all lose faith' (Mk 14:29), but Matthew has Peter indicate *why* they might fall away: 'Though all lose faith *in you*' (Mt 26:33). Mark associates the rest of the disciples with Peter's profession of loyalty in general terms: 'And they all said the same' (Mk 14:31), but Matthew makes specific to 'all the disciples' as he reports: 'And all the disciples said the same' (Mt 26:35).

While Matthew looks to the work which was the major source for his Gospel, the earlier Gospel of Mark, and basically repeats the account of the events of the night before Jesus died, he is able to tell it for his own Church in his own way. There was a need in the Matthean Church to associate failing disciples with Jesus. At the eucharistic table, the members of the Matthean community recalled in their sinfulness that the founding disciples who prefigure the Matthean Church also failed. Indeed, Matthew's slight but significant reinterpretation of the Markan version of the story focuses its attention even more closely upon the fact that it was, above all, the disciples who failed. It is to failing disciples that Jesus commands: 'Take it and eat' (Mt 26:26) and 'Drink all of you from this' (26:27).

The scene in Gethsemane and the arrest of Jesus, leading to the flight of the disciples largely follows the traditional story. However, as is to be expected, some uniquely Matthean points are made. As Jesus prays to his Father, his awareness that he is following the will of the Father in the fulfilment of his plans is made more clear: 'My Father, if this cup cannot pass by without my drinking it, your will be done' (26:42). As Jesus had earlier taught his disciples to pray to the Father, so now he does himself: 'Your will be done' (see Mt 6:10). The point is made even more strongly as Jesus replies to his captors in the garden: 'Do you think that I cannot appeal to my Father who would promptly send more than twelve legions of angels to my defence? But then how would the scriptures be fulfilled that say this is the way it must be? . . . I sat teaching in the Temple day after day and you never laid hands on me.' Matthew then comments: 'Now all this happened to fulfil the prophecies in scripture' (26:53-56).

After this comment Matthew immediately reports: 'Then all the disciples deserted him and ran away' (v. 26b). Jesus will go into the paschal events alone, as he alone will return to his failed disciples, sending them out to the ends of the earth (28:16-20). Again we must ask: what happens between these two events?

The Jewish trial concentrates on an ironic presentation of Jesus as the Christ and the Son of God. His accusers will proclaim the truth as they insist that Jesus made blasphemous claims. Indeed, the demands of the High Priest repeat the titles used by Peter earlier in the Gospel to answer correctly Jesus' question, 'Who do you say I am?' (see 16:15-16): 'I put you on oath by the living God to tell us if you are the Christ, the Son of God' (26:63). As Peter's confession was created by Jesus' question about the Son of Man (see 16:13), so at the trial Jesus corrects the High Priest by telling him of the Son of Man who 'from this time onward' shall be seen as seated on his throne. The passion — apparently an ignominious death — is in fact the place and the time where Jesus will establish the kingdom of his Father.

While both Mark and Matthew report Peter's denials, only Matthew adds the scene of Judas' despair. Matthew insists more than Mark that Peter was with Jesus (see 26:69, 71), and then that 'You are *one of them* for sure!' (v. 73). As the denials intensify, they eventually produce a curse: 'Then he started calling down curses upon himself and swearing, 'I do not know the man' (26:74). A disciple has lost Jesus, and thus he has lost his place as a disciple. But he repents: 'And he went outside and wept bitterly' (v. 75).

The reader immediately reads on to find the story of Judas, which only Matthew reports. Side by side with the sinful Peter who repents we find the further story of the other possibility for a disciple who loses Jesus through his sinfulness: despair and suicide (27:1-10). The Sanhedrin cares little for the human tragedy of Judas, they worry about the ritual uncleanliness created by the blood money, and in their callous misunderstanding of all that has happened, they unwittingly fulfil the scriptures (27:6-10). Matthew has placed the stories of Peter and Judas to address Christians, especially Christian leaders, about the possibilities open to them in their failure. To resort to a ritual cleanliness overlooks the essential question of one's relationship with the person of Jesus. Thus, the sinful Christian is left with two options: repentance (Peter) and despair (Judas).

If the trial before the Jewish authorities recalled and reinforced Jesus' claims as Messiah and the suffering Son of Man who would return as judge, the trial before Pilate and the crucifixion scene concentrate upon titles of honour, especially 'King' and 'Son'. The first words Pilate utters are: 'Are you the king of the Jews' (27:11), and Jesus' kingship runs through the whole of the scene (see vv. 11, 17, 22, 29, 37, 42). Once Jesus has been crucified, his tormentors say: 'If you are God's son, come down from the Cross' (v. 40), and the theme of Jesus' 'sonship' is explicitly restated in vv. 43 and 54.

Pilate attempts to free Jesus by asking the Jews to choose between Jesus and Barabbas, and his wife's pleas add to this theme. Gentiles plead for Jesus as the Jewish leaders urge the crowds to ask for Barabbas, rather than the King of the Jews. It is within this context that Matthew makes his most important addition to the trial before Pilate. In vv. 24-25 the key word is 'blood'. Pilate washes his hands and claims: 'I am innocent of this man's blood. It is your concern'. And all the people answered, 'His blood be on us and on our children'. The Jewish leaders tried to wash their hands of the blood of Jesus by not using the blood money which Judas had flung back at them (see 27:3-10). Pilate also tries to wash his hands of the blood of Jesus. The responsibility for the blood of Jesus is accepted by the people. Earlier in the Gospel, after speaking of the many prophets rejected and slain in Israel, Jesus prophesied: 'You will draw down on yourselves the blood of every holy man that has been shed on earth, from the blood of Abel the Holy to the blood of Zecharaiah the son of Barachiah, whom you murdered between the sanctuary and the altar. I tell you solemnly, all of this will recoil on this generation' (23:35-36).

An angry relationship existed between the members of Matthew's Christian community and their fellow-Jews from the Synagogue across the road who had ejected them because they believed in Jesus as the Christ, but there is more to it. The words of 'all the people' forms part of the turning point of the ages which will take place in the death and resurrection of Jesus. The Kingdom of God is taken from this people and given to another people, the Church, which will bear good fruit. Again, words of Jesus addressed to the crowds earlier in the Gospel are recalled: 'The kingdom of God will be taken away from you and given to a people who will bear its fruits' (21:43). The status of 'God's chosen people' is shifting away from Israel to the Church. While earlier in the Gospel Jesus had commanded that the mission could only be to the 'lost sheep of the House of Israel' (10:6), now we are approaching a moment in God's history where Jesus will be able to command a mission to 'all the nations' (28:19). The measure of being God's people no longer depends upon nationhood or blood line, but upon preparedness to accept Jesus as Messiah, Son of Man, King and Son of God. Israel refuses to accept him as such.

The scene of the death of Jesus introduces some surprising new elements only found in Matthew which prove that the ironical proclamation contained in the insult hurled at him by 'the passers-by' and by the chief priests and the scribes is true. In fact, those who 'had finished crucifying him', and who then 'sat down and stayed there keeping guard over there' (27:36) will come to see the truth of the insults. In his account of the death of Jesus

Matthew carries further his claim that 'the turning point of the ages' has come.

There is a series of signs which come from a Jewish understanding of the end of time. The prophet Amos had spoken of the day of the Lord (the end time), saying: 'On that day God will make the sun set at noon and will cover the earth with darkness in broad daylight' (Amos 8:9). And so it is as Jesus dies: 'From the sixth hour there was darkness over all the land until the ninth hour' (v. 45). Matching the fearful darkness is Jesus' cry: 'My God, my God, why have you deserted me?' (v. 46). The just man abandons himself completely to God in a mixture of anguish and filial trust. Misunderstanding 'Eli' (my God) as 'Elijah' (the prophet) the bystanders will not admit what Jesus has said or who he is (v. 49). As they wait to see if Elijah will come to his aid, he cries out again and 'yielded up his spirit' (v. 50).

Without any introduction, or reason, a further series of events is described:

> 'At that, the veil of the Temple was torn from top to bottom; the earth quaked; the rocks were split; the tombs opened and the bodies of many holy men rose from the dead, and these, after his resurrection, came out of the tombs, entered the Holy City and appeared to a number of people' (vv. 51-53).

Why is it important for Matthew suddenly to introduce the report of these strange events at this stage of his story? He is telling his readers that history has reached its turning point with the death of Jesus. At the beginning of his teaching, Jesus had said: 'Until heaven and earth disappear, not one dot, not one little stroke, shall disappear from the Law until its purpose is achieved' (Mt 5:18). That 'until' is being fulfilled: heaven and earth are passing away. This is the meaning of the signs and wonders which God works as Jesus dies (Mt 27: 51-54). The events which *only Matthew* associated with the death of Jesus belonged to a series of signs from the apocalyptic symbolism of the Old Testament (see Ps 114:7-8; Is 48:21; Nahum 1:5-6 and especially Ezek 37:1-14 and Dan 12:2). They were used in the Old Testament to describe the end time and the ultimate power of God. However, the 'end of time' in these Old Testament passages meant exactly that — when all history would come to an end, when heaven and earth will pass away. Matthew has taken traditional signs and located them in time, in the story of Jesus.

The darkening of the skies, the shaking of the earth and the splitting open of the rocks proclaim the turning point of the ages. Already at the death of Jesus we are told of the resurrection of the holy ones: 'Many holy men rose from the dead . . . came out of the tombs, entered the Holy City and appeared to a number of people' (v. 53). This is Matthew's way of affirming that, with the death of Jesus, a new age has broken into the old. Judaism and its cult have come to an end (the Temple veil is torn apart). The way to God is open to all.

At the cross, while death and sin are conquered, Matthew further shows that all the Old Testament restrictions of race, cult and law are thrown down. This is the point of v. 54. Picking up the earlier indications of v. 36, in reference to those who had nailed him to a cross, abused him, and who sat about watching over him, Matthew now writes:

> 'Meanwhile the centurion, together with the others guarding Jesus, had seen the earthquake and all that was taking place, and they were terrified and said, 'In truth this was a son of God' ' (v. 54)

In Matthew it is not only the centurion, but also 'the others guarding Jesus' who are forced to a confession of the sonship of Jesus in the light of the world shattering events which have accompanied his death. The soldiers standing with the centurion were the people who nailed

Jesus to the cross, who divided his garments and who mocked him. The gathering of 'all nations' (see 28:19) into the Church is foreshadowed here, as soldiers look upon the criminal they have crucified, and proclaim him as the Son of God.

Thus, in 27:40 the Jews mock Jesus on the cross wagging their heads and jeering: 'If you are God's son, come down from the cross'. Now the non-Jews, soldiers and centurion, proclaim: 'In truth, this was a son of God' (v. 54). Profoundly important themes intermingle here. The request from the Jewish onlookers reflects a crisis facing any believer who would have Jesus' Sonship conform to human criteria. It would seem impossible that the crucified one could be the Son of God. Yet, that is God's way: to separate Jesus from the cross would be to deny his Sonship. He is Son of God (v. 54) because he did not 'come down from the cross' (v. 40). A new age has begun, and its first fruits are a Gentile centurion and his company. They see the signs of the new age — 'the earthquake and all that was taking place' — and they proclaim the crucified Jesus as the Son of God (v. 54).

The resurrection of Jesus will be marked by similar world-shattering events (see 28:2-4). The death of Jesus on the Cross initiates the turning point of the ages. For the moment we rest with the first act of a conflict between the truthfulness of the early Christian witness to Jesus' resurrection, and the lies of the Jewish authorities who suspect that his disciples might steal the body (see 27:62-68; 28:11-15). In the end the truth will be proclaimed (see 28:7), and Jesus will send his Church out to the ends of the earth (28:16-20). The story of Jesus' passion, as it is told in the Gospel of Matthew, relentlessly portrays the suffering of Jesus. But it also points us forward towards the Resurrection and the future life of the Church.

THE SEASON OF EASTER

EASTER NIGHT

Matthew 28:1-10

Dawn of the first day of the week

The passion and death of Jesus initiated a process through which the old order was passing away and a new was dawning. At the death of Jesus Matthew reports that many strange events took place: darkness, earthquake and holy people rising from their tombs. Similar events occur in Matthew's story of the resurrection of Jesus.

'Towards dawn on the first day of the week', the women who had stood firm through the tragedy of the Cross, Mary of Magdala and the other Mary (Mt 28:1. See 27:61) go to visit the sepulchre of Jesus. The setting of the following events 'towards dawn' on the first of all Easter Sundays promises the reader that the women will find more than a sepulchre. A new light is breaking into the darkness of night.

For a moment the women on their journey are forgotten, as a series of 'end-time' events are reported as happening at the tomb (vv. 2-4). In a way similar to the events surrounding Jesus' death on the Cross, there is a violent earthquake. An angel of the Lord descends from heaven, rolls away the stone and sits upon it. Through his angel, God enters the story. The description of the angel, 'his face was like lightning, his robe white as snow', adds to the terror of the moment and the guards, collapse to the ground like dead men. At the Cross the Gentiles came to faith in Jesus (see 27:54), here the guards are part of the description of an anticipated 'end-time'.

The angel speaks to the women, assuring them that they need not fear. They need no longer search for the crucified one. He has been raised. The tomb, the place of death, is empty. However, it is not enough simply to gaze in awe at an empty tomb. The women are commissioned to carry the Easter proclamation to the disciples: 'Go quickly and tell his disciples, "He has risen from the dead, and now he is going before you into Galilee, it is there you will see him"' (vv. 5-7).

The women recognise they have been touched by the action of God: it is the reason for their awe. They are also filled with great joy at the privilege given to them. But on their way back to the disciples, the risen Jesus meets them and they fall down and cling to him. He greets them, and repeats almost exactly the same message as the angel, commissioning the disciples to go into Galilee. However, there is an important difference. While the angel told them to speak to Jesus' *disciples*, Jesus himself refers to them as *my brethren*. It is not failed disciples who must go to Galilee; it is a group of people who once again belong to the family of Jesus.

Earlier in the Gospel the disciples had forsaken Jesus and fled (see 26:56). All such failures have now been forgiven. The broken bond has been healed. The resurrection of Jesus has completed the turning point of the ages which began with his death. Now the women are filled with great joy; now the sinful disciples are restored to the family of Jesus. Shortly he will indeed meet them in Galilee, to send them out to the whole world (see 28:16-20).

May Easter lead us to awe and joy as we recognise the greatness of our God who raised his Son to life that we too might have life, no matter how often and how seriously we have fled from him.

EASTER SUNDAY

John 20:1-9

Reading the signs of victory over death

While the Synoptic Gospels set the journey of the women to the tomb of Jesus at the dawn of the first day of the week, the Fourth Evangelist moves away from that tradition. He deliberately sets the scene for an initial lack of faith, by reporting that when Mary Magdala came to the tomb 'it was very early . . . and still dark' (John 20:1). Any reader familiar with the Fourth Gospel will be aware that 'darkness' symbolises the absence of Jesus, and even hostility to the light which he has come to bring.

Mary sees the 'sign' of an empty tomb: the stone is rolled away. Empty tombs are not 'good news'. She reads this particular empty tomb as 'bad news', rushing back to the disciples — *away* from the place of Jesus' victory over death — to announce: 'They have taken the Lord out of the tomb' (v.2). While Mary is prepared to speak of the crucified Jesus as 'the Lord', she is only thinking of him as the man she once knew and loved so well, but who is now buried in a tomb. There is no hint or suggestion that Jesus may have been raised: our Easter Gospel begins with an unbelieving Mary.

This news sends Peter and 'the other disciple, the one whom Jesus loved' running *back towards* the tomb (vv. 3-4). They reverse Mary Magdala's flight. Although Mary has not been able to read the sign of the empty tomb, her message has set other disciples in motion towards that sign. A journey to faith has begun. Indeed, the disciple who has been loved by the Lord is powerfully drawn towards the 'signs' of the tomb. Although recognising Peter's authority on arrival, he outruns him on the journey (v. 4).

Peter sees the cloths which had previously wrapped the crucified body of the Lord, separated and folded neatly in different places in the tomb (vv. 5-7). We are not told of Peter's reaction, but the reader recalls the resurrection of Lazarus. When Lazarus was raised from death, he still wore the clothes of death (11:44). This is not the case for Jesus. Whatever may have been the reaction of Peter, the Beloved Disciple enters, sees the same 'signs': the empty tomb and the folded cloths, and comes to faith: 'He saw and he believed' (20:8). Only now disciples grasp that the scriptures, teaching that Jesus must rise from the dead, have been fulfilled. The darkness of unbelief which began this account — 'it was very early, and still dark' — has now been turned into the light of faith.

John has chosen to tell his Easter story by reporting the mixed reactions of the first people who heard the message and saw the signs. They were the foundational members of the Christian community: Mary Magdalene, Peter and the Beloved Disciple. Resurrection faith did not come instantaneously. Even these first disciples, both women and men, made *their* journey from no faith to complete faith through their experience of the 'signs' that Jesus has been victorious over death. The realities of death, tomb and cloths, cannot contain him.

The same journey from darkness to light is available to all of us. The signs of the risen Lord among us are not physical, but they are there: care and loyalty in love, courage and commitment, faithfulness, and the great joy which comes from our Christian faith. Easter invites us to read these and the many other 'signs' of the risen Lord among us.

SECOND SUNDAY OF EASTER

John 20:19-31

Sent by the risen Lord

Both of the events recorded in today's Gospel take place on 'the first day of the week' (Jn 20:19, 26). The events which take place on the Day of the Lord stand at the heart of the Christian Church and its mission. We recall and make present these events in our Sunday celebration.

Disciples are locked in the upper room, fearful of what might happen to them (Jn 20:19). Somehow, the Beloved Disciple's coming to faith at the empty tomb has not moved the rest of the group to abandon their 'fear of the Jews'. But the Jesus whom they saw crucified comes to them alive, bringing them peace in the midst of their fear. 'The disciples were filled with joy when they saw the Lord' (v. 20).

Having transformed their fear into joy, Jesus then sends the disciples out as his missionaries. Throughout the Gospel of John, Jesus has both been described and described himself as the one sent by the Father. Now this mission is passed down to the next generation: 'As the Father sent me, so I am sending you' (v. 21). The coming of the risen Jesus has dispelled all fear. His gift of the Spirit to them will enable them to continue this mission of the Son. They are to bring peace and to dispel fear as they become the sent ones of the Son. By forgiving sin as a result of the gift of the Spirit, the Christian disciple of all time will also overcome the fear and the pain which slavery to sin inevitably produces (vv. 22-23).

However, one of the disciples was not there. When the disciples came to faith and joy, and received the commission to bring the peace and healing of Jesus into the world — Thomas was not present (v. 24). Informed that Jesus is alive, it is not that Thomas will not believe; he will, but only in his own way. Jesus must meet his conditions and expectations: '*Unless* I see the holes that the nails made . . . *unless* I can put my hand into his side' (v. 25). Thomas demands tangible evidence of the passion. How can a dead man be alive again?

The following Day of the Lord ('eight days later' [v. 26]) the risen Jesus again comes to the group of disciples both to show the limitations of Thomas' demands and to lead him to a confession of true Christian faith which no longer depends upon tangible proof. The pierced body, offered to Thomas, is evidence that the crucified Jesus is now the risen Lord. The only response to such a life-giving presence is Thomas' recognition of who it is that he dared to question: 'My Lord and my God'.

But Thomas is not the end of the story. Many Sundays later, we are being asked to recognise the greatness of the gift we have been given: 'You believe because you can see me. Happy are those who have not seen and yet believe' (v. 29). As we celebrate our Sunday liturgy we can rightly claim that we have not seen, and yet we believe. May the ongoing story of our Christian journey always show that our belief in Jesus as the Christ, the Son of God, has given us life in his name (vv. 30-31). Filled with such life we will, however modestly, repeat the mission of Jesus. As the Father sent him, so now he is sending us. At times we will also repeat the Thomas story, demanding that Jesus meet our expectations. May Jesus' never-failing presence to us also lead us to confess 'My Lord and my God'.

THIRD SUNDAY OF EASTER

Luke 24:13-35

The breaking of the bread

Jesus' decision to go up to Jerusalem forms a turning point in Luke's story of Jesus. The Evangelist reports solemnly: 'Now as the time drew near for him to be taken up to heaven, he resolutely took the road for Jerusalem' (Lk 9:51). After a long journey (see 9:51-19:44), during which Jesus forms his disciples for their future mission and enters into deeper and deeper conflict with the powers that oppose him, he comes to Jerusalem (19:45). Once in Jerusalem, he never leaves the Holy City.

God makes himself known in the events which have taken place in Jerusalem: the suffering, death and resurrection of Jesus. But two disciples decided they have had enough of the journey to Jerusalem and all the events which occurred there. They are walking to Emmaus: seven miles *away from* Jerusalem (24:13). They are leaving the place of God's presence to them, they are leaving the pivot of God's salvation history.

The risen Lord sets out to journey with them (v. 15). On the journey the travellers tell Jesus, whom they suggest must be the only person in Jerusalem who does not know what has taken place there (v. 18), that they know everything. Indeed, they know all the *facts* about Jesus. They know of Jesus' life as a wonder worker, as a teacher and they have experienced his cruel death. They even know of a visit of women to a tomb which they found empty, and they have heard of the message of the angels: 'He is alive', and they tell Jesus 'two whole days have gone by' (v. 21). It is now the third day.

But with all this knowledge and experience, they did not see Jesus. They have their ideas: 'Our own hope had been that he would be the one to set Israel free' (v. 21). This is the reason for their inability to see Jesus. They have made up their own minds about who Jesus is and what he should have done for the nation. Because the freedom which the risen Jesus brings is greater than anything they were hoping for, they are unable to see him.

However Jesus does not abandon the two disciples. He journeys with them, and instructs them through the Scriptures, showing them that it was necessary for the Messiah to suffer and die (vv. 25-27). At the end of the day, he pretends to go on. They must now play their part and they invite him to stay with them (vv. 28-29). At table 'he took the bread and said the blessing; then he broke it and handed it to them' (v. 30). The wandering disciples recognise the Lord in the breaking of the bread, and immediately return to Jerusalem, which they should never have left (v. 33). Indeed, arriving in Jerusalem full of their news, they discover that 'the Lord has risen and has appeared to Simon' (vv. 33-34). The disciples who had never left Jerusalem know already. The wandering disciples have come home.

How often do we find that the demands of the Lord are too much for us? We too walk away from our Jerusalem, where the action of God can be difficult to cope with, especially as it sometimes runs contrary to our own hopes. Reading the story of the breaking of the bread at Emmaus we are strengthened in our faltering faith. Jesus sets out to walk with his wandering disciples of all times. He instructs, and he breaks bread with us . . . and in this way he leads us home.

FOURTH SUNDAY OF EASTER

John 10:1-10

Shepherds and brigands

We easily identify Jesus with the Good Shepherd, on the basis of the many other things we know about his life, his teaching, and his loving gift of himself, even unto death. It comes as a surprise, therefore, to know that this first part of the Gospel of the Good Shepherd, read in today's liturgy, does not at all apply the shepherd image to Jesus.

Jesus explains that some have come to steal, slaughter and destroy, but there are others whose presence enables abundant life (v. 10). The background to this imagery is the prophet Ezekiel who had spoken sternly to the leaders of Israel. They should have been the shepherds of the people, but instead they abandoned them, looking after their own interests, leading the flock, the people of Israel, into slaughter (see Ezek 34:1-10).

There are bad leaders and there are good leaders. The good leader of God's people must come to them through Jesus. There is only one way to enter into the sheepfold to bring wholeness and life to a flock which will recognise the shepherd who calls his sheep by name: through the gate. Such a shepherd leads the flock into good pastures. The shepherds of God's people who are prepared to come through Jesus will be all that Christian leaders should be, for only Jesus can claim 'I am the Way, the Truth and the Life' (Jn 14:6).

The thief and the brigand who do not enter through the gate only lead the flock into a situation where they will be scattered, running away in fear. Now that they are out of the fold and running in fear, their destiny can only be tragedy and slaughter. Such a situation results from a leadership which comes to God's people with its own plans, its own agenda and its own career in mind.

Jesus' listeners were not able to understand what he was telling them through this parable. His explanation may come as a surprise to us. Jesus does not claim to be the good shepherd. He says: 'I am the gate of the sheepfold . . . I am the gate . . . Anyone who enters through me'. Paying attention to this detail leads us to understand that the good shepherd is not Jesus. The good shepherd is a Church which does indeed call each sheep by name, and which leads a flock which knows its voice. Of course, there is a sense in which Jesus is also the Good Shepherd, and therefore the model of the Church, but that point is made later in John 10, in association with his death (see vv. 14-15).

Today we are challenged as Church, just as we are challenged as members of the Lord's flock. As Church do we tend the flock given into our care (family, parish, friends, those who look to us for love, care and guidance) by passing through the gate which is Jesus and the way of his Gospel, or have we developed our own way of doing things? Are we shepherds as Jesus is the Good Shepherd, laying down his life for his sheep (v. 15)?

As members of the Lord's flock, living in the midst of a world which has forgotten its Lord, can we frankly say that we 'do not recognise the voice of strangers', but that we listen only to the voice which we know? Do we really know that voice of the good shepherd, or are the sounds of the many thieves and brigands at large in today's society too loud in our ears?

FIFTH SUNDAY OF EASTER

John 14:1-12

The departure of Jesus

Today's Gospel draws our attention to Jesus' departure, and to the attitude of the disciple in the new era. It opens with a two-fold command: 'Trust in God still and trust in me' (Jn 14:1), and it closes with the same message: 'Do you not believe that I am in the Father and the Father is in me? . . . You must believe me . . . believe it on the evidence of this work . . . Whoever believes in me . . . will perform even greater works' (vv. 10, 11, 12). In this way the theme for the passage is set. Jesus must return to his Father, and thus leave the disciples in the world to continue the task which Jesus has begun.

However, there is a way of life which will give the disciple guidance and courage: the way of faith. But there is more than guidance and courage involved. Not only will the believing disciples continue the presence of Jesus in the world; they will 'perform even greater works' (v. 12). The Church does not simply repeat what Jesus did. It lives through the centuries, facing new challenges, translating the words and ways of Jesus into new situations and new demands upon the Gospel which it preaches.

How is all this possible? The answer is supplied in the words of Jesus which come between his two exhortations to faith. Jesus tells of his place in the Father's plan. The departure of Jesus from his followers is a temporary measure, a necessary journey away from us so that one day he will be able to come back and lead us to his Father's house (vv. 2-3). In the meantime, we should know the way to the place where he is going (v. 4).

Therein lies the problem: Philip voices our complaint in saying that we do not know the way (v. 5). But we should: Jesus is the way, the truth and the life (v. 6). We are called to adopt his way, his life-style, his approach to God and to humankind and creation. This is the only Way which can be described as truth and life. It responds to the deepest stirrings of our spirit, leading us to a knowledge of the one true God (vv. 7-10). Jesus is not among us as a physical person whom we can consult, look at and follow in the physical sense. But he is always among us as the way, the truth and the life.

Our God and Father has made himself known in the life-story of Jesus (v. 10). Jesus primarily describes himself as 'the way'. The words 'the truth and the life' are used to describe 'the way' (v. 6). In Jesus we can discover God's way in the world, a way which brings truth and life. To do greater things than Jesus, we must rediscover the purpose and the driving force behind Jesus' life-story.

There are many 'ways of life' which are daily thrust before us as the 'way to success'. But, as the great success-stories of this world come and go, rise and fall, live and die, the word and way of Jesus are always with us. If we await his return guided by the way he lived and loved, then we will enjoy the presence of both Jesus and his Father empowering us to do even greater things than Jesus. The success of what we do depends upon our faith and trust in him. Following Jesus the way, we Christians will bring the truth and life which continue to give direction to those who have become lost or puzzled in the confusions of our difficult world.

SIXTH SUNDAY OF EASTER

John 14:15-21

If you love me

The theme of the departure of Jesus continues into this Sunday's Gospel. The readings of these Sundays are set within the upper room and they all describe the final evening which Jesus spent with his disciples. His opening words to them would be a challenge: 'If you love me' (Jn 14:15). Of course the disciples thought they loved Jesus: they would not be there with him unless they did. The same could be said of us as we attend our Sunday liturgy. But this means that we must be prepared to accept the following imperative: 'You will keep my commandments' (v. 15).

To claim to love Jesus necessarily implies that we must live according to his commandments. This may frighten us, aware as we are of our frailty. But the call to follow his commandments is, encouragingly, accompanied by a gift; the gift of another Advocate. It is important to see that Jesus speaks of *another* Advocate. The first Advocate is Jesus himself. Now that he is about to leave the disciples, he sends another, to stand with us during the interim time between his two comings.

Jesus was the first one to counsel and guide us. He showed that 'God so loved the world that he sent his only Son' (3:16). The Son shows us how much God loves us, and asks us to love just as he has loved. These are the basic truths which lie behind Jesus' commandment: 'What I command you is to love one another' (15:17). The gift of the Spirit is a further gift to ensure that the commandment of love will be observed among the followers of Jesus. There are two great gifts: the Father's gift of the Son and the Son's gift of the Spirit.

Jesus will not leave us orphans and will eventually come back (v. 18). In the meantime we are asked to respond by loving one another as he has loved us, guided, strengthened and enlightened by the Spirit of truth who will be with us forever (v. 17). There is a way of living our human story which corresponds to the way Jesus lived his. With his ongoing presence among us through the Spirit, the commandments of Jesus which call us to his way of loving are possible.

Too often the Christian ideal of love is watered down. Christian love is not a comfortable feeling of 'warm fuzziness'. Nor does it consist in untroubled deep and meaningful exchanges of 'how we really feel' which some dream to be at the heart of Christian community. The Christian community is not a group of psychologically complete and mature human beings who always relate in the most perfect fashion. This has never been the case and never will be. If it were, then Jesus' commandment to love would be meaningless.

Today's Gospel tells us that the Christian life of love calls for an active involvement in a broken world which God loved so much that he sent his Son to save it. There is a mystery into which Christian life has been plunged. Jesus has shown us the Father's love in his gift of himself for us, despite our personal messiness and the complexity of the world in which we live and relate. We are now called to repeat that love. 'Impossible!', says a self-centred society which only ever asks: 'What's in it for me?'. However, it is possible for us because we are not alone. The gift of Jesus' Spirit is with us to guide and to instruct.

THE ASCENSION OF THE LORD

Matthew 28:16-20

Jesus present among us

The celebration of the Ascension marks Jesus' physical separation from the human story. But today's Gospel announces that he is with us always (Mt 28:20). Even before he was born, the angel said to Joseph that he would be called Emmanuel, a name which means 'God is with us' (see 1:23). If today we celebrate Jesus' departure, how is he still with us?

Today's Gospel tells us. Going to the top of the mountain, Jesus chooses a traditional site for closeness to God for these final words to his disciples, as he had done at the beginning of his ministry as he taught them on the mountain (5:1—7:28). The disciples, who have never wholly accepted all that Jesus asked them to believe and do, recognise him and fall to the ground as a sign of their acceptance of him. However, despite their outward sign of faith, some still hesitated (v. 17). This is typical of disciples of all times. To believe is one thing, but to live according to the demands which follow true belief in Jesus can cause us to hesitate.

Addressing the believing but fragile disciples, the risen Jesus explains how he is and always will be present to the new people of God, founded by faith in him, no matter how hesitant. What was once the privilege of JHWH, the God of Israel, has now been given to Jesus: 'All authority in heaven and on earth has been given to me (v. 18). Jesus claims to be the presence of the living God in our story. Because this is true, he is able to issue three commands which ensure that he will be among us always.

He first breaks through all the limitations of race for the new People of God. Disciples are to be made from 'all the nations'. Gone is the reservation of that privilege to the people of Israel. He next instructs his future missionaries on a new initiation rite: baptism in the name of the Father, the Son and the Holy Spirit (v. 19). While once only males could be properly introduced into the fulness of life in the People of God through circumcision, now the universal possibility of baptism is offered to all nations and to all people, women and men.

Finally, Jesus replaces the sacred Law of Israel. While once the People of God had to observe all the commandments of Moses, now a new people will be formed on the basis of the teaching of Jesus. The missionaries are to teach everyone to observe the commands which Jesus gave (v. 20).

We celebrate Jesus' departure as an Ascension. But he is still among us. All that had been a rich and empowering presence of JHWH to Israel, their nation, their initiation and the Law, has been surpassed. Jesus is present among us in a Church which opens its doors to all nations, bringing them life through the waters of baptism, instructing them in the teachings of Jesus. But it is not primarily the institutional Church which must do this. We are the disciples who believe, but hesitate; we are the disciples invited to recognise Jesus still among us, and challenged to take his presence to all peoples and all places. The Ascension is not a departure. It is a challenge to bring Jesus, still among us, to a world that does not know him, however Christian it may sometimes call itself.

PENTECOST

John 20:19-23

Transformation

The setting for this Gospel reading is the same as that of the several Gospels which we read during the Easter Season: the upper room. On the evening before his death Jesus instructed his disciples that he had to depart to his Father, that he would not leave them orphans, that they must continue his presence in the world by loving as he had loved, and that he would give them the Spirit to guide, teach and support them in their trials. All this now seems to be forgotten.

The disciples are locked in the upper room, fearful of what might happen to them at the hands of 'the Jews' (Jn 20:15). 'The Jews' had slain Jesus . . . what might they do to his disciples? But the Jesus whom they had seen nailed hand and foot to a Cross comes to them — alive! The man who had been agonizingly crucified is not only alive, but he comes to bring peace. The violence of the darkness which attempted in vain to quench the light (see 1:5) has produced peace. On two occasions he greets them: 'Peace be with you' (vv. 20, 21). On the basis of the transformation which occurred through the resurrection of the crucified one a similar process can take place in the disciples.

'The disciples were filled with joy when they saw the Lord' (v. 20). Death has turned into life and peace, and thus the disciples' fear turns into joy. Here we find the beginnings of the transformation which the death and resurrection of Jesus can produce. But the presence of the risen Lord in his Church is not only a presence which brings peace and joy; it is also a presence which brings responsibility.

As the Father had sent him, so now he sends the disciples (v. 21), but the promises he made in the upper room must first be fulfilled. He gives them the Spirit, the other Advocate who would stand by them, instruct them and strengthen them (vv. 22-23). The disciples have been further transformed. With the gift of the Spirit, fear is turned into joy. The disciple now becomes the missionary. Jesus, the sent one of the Father has overcome their fearfulness. They are now commissioned to repeat the same transforming task. By forgiving sin as a result of the gift of the Spirit, the Christian disciple will also overcome the fear and the pain which slavery to sin inevitably produces (v. 23). The disciples have been empowered to transform. The wholeness and holiness which Jesus' gift of the Spirit has brought into the lives of the disciples are now available, through them, to the forgiven sinner.

Pentecost puts an end to fear. The gift of the Spirit must give us the courage to open doors we lock around us. The Christian Church must take a serious look at itself and its performance. How are we coping with the increasingly complicated and godless world into which Jesus sends us? Have we closed the doors around us, forming an elite, happy that we have all the answers? We need to be transformed at Pentecost. Our fear must be turned into joy, the disciple must become the missionary, opening doors that we have shut. Repeating the mission of Jesus himself, we have now been sent, not to judge the world, but to save it (see Jn 3:16).

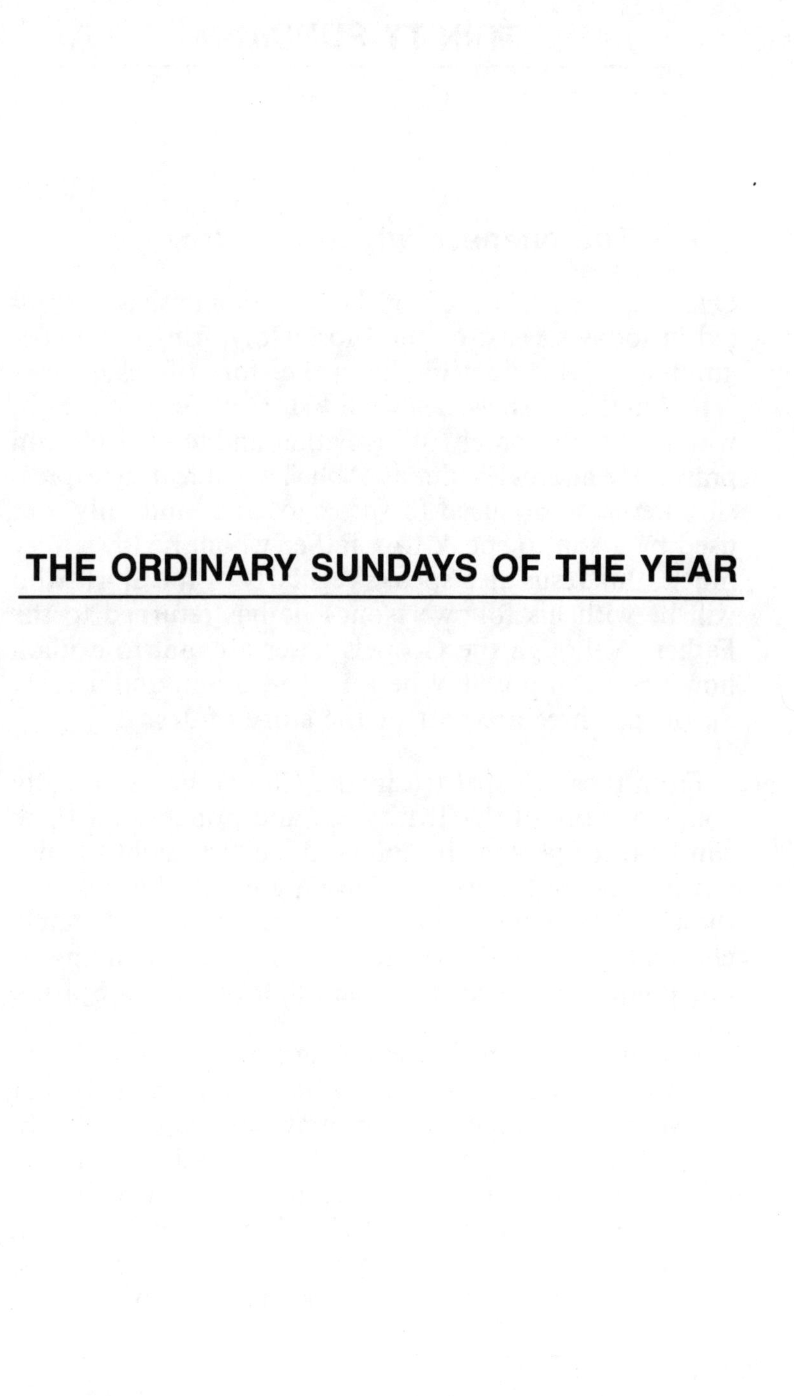

THE ORDINARY SUNDAYS OF THE YEAR

TRINITY SUNDAY

John 3:16-18

The oneness which love creates

One of the central beliefs of the Christian faith is celebrated in today's Feast of the Most Holy Trinity. The beginnings of this doctrine lie in the story of Jesus, as it is told in the Gospels. They tell a story of Jesus, the Son, who speaks intimately of his Father and to his Father in prayer. He addresses him as 'Abba', an endearing expression never before used to speak to God, and only ever used by a son to speak to a father whom he loves very much. But Jesus also speaks regularly of the Spirit who will be with his followers once he has returned to the Father. Although the Gospels never attempt to explain how there can possibly be a Father, a Son and a Holy Spirit, all three are part of the story of Jesus.

From these Gospel truths the Church has eventually come to speak of the Trinity . . . and wonder how there can be three persons in one God. At first sight today's Gospel may not appear to have a great deal to do with the mystery of the Trinity, but it has been deliberately chosen to give us the key to a proper understanding of our unique God who is Father, Son and Holy Spirit.

Everything begins in the loving action of a God who loved the world so much that he sent his Son so that everyone who believes in him may have eternal life (Jn 3:16). There is only one motive for the Father's sending of his Son: love. But what does it mean 'to believe in him . . . to believe in the name of God's only Son'? It would be a mistake to think, as many have over the centuries, that such belief is an intellectual assent to a set of dogmas.

There is only one place where we can discover the love which motivated the Father to send his Son — in the love which the Son showed both for his Father and for us. As the Letter of John says: 'God is love. In this the love of God was made manifest among us, that God sent his only Son into the world' (1 Jn 4:8-9). To 'believe in' the Son, the manifestation of God's love in the world, is to allow ourselves to be caught up in the same divine reality: love. Deep in our hearts we know that this is what we yearn for, no matter how often we thwart our longings.

It is often pointed out that, for the Gospel of John, there is no judgment at the end of time. We judge ourselves as we either accept or refuse the love of God made known to us in the person, the teaching and the death and resurrection of Jesus. This is what is implied in the words of Jesus: 'No one who believes in him will be condemned; but whoever refuses to believe is condemned already' (Jn 3:18). The Father makes his love known to us through his Son. Are we prepared to accept this Son?

The Father, who is love, has a Son whom he loves, yet gives to the world so that we might come to understand love. But all that happened nearly two thousand years ago. How are we touched by God's love, shown to us in his Son? The loving union between the Father and the Son which has broken into our story is the Spirit, very much alive among us as a Church, and touching the profoundest depths in each one of us. The Spirit renders present the love of God shown to us in Jesus. Restless are our hearts, dear Lord, until they rest in you. To believe in a God who is Father, Son and Holy Spirit is to place all our trust and hope in a oneness which only love can create.

THE BODY AND BLOOD OF CHRIST

John 6:51-58

Flesh for the life of the world

Today's Gospel reading forms part of a longer passage in the Gospel of John. After Jesus had multiplied the bread, fed the masses (Jn 6:1-15) and come to his disciples across a stormy sea, revealing himself with the words: 'It is I. Do not be afraid' (v. 20. See vv. 16-21), a crowd gathers at Capernaum (vv. 22-25). He speaks at length to them about the gift of the true bread from heaven which only Jesus can give (vv. 25-50). Jewish thought made much of Moses' having given his people bread from heaven during the Exodus (see v. 31), but the bread which Jesus gives surpasses the bread given by the Fathers of Israel (vv. 49-50).

Jesus' listeners had also often heard of God's gift of wisdom which would nourish the people. In fact, they often looked back to Moses' gift of bread and linked it with the gift of the Law, the supreme Wisdom which gave life to those who lived by it. The notion of a bread which gives life was not new to the disciples and the Jewish crowd. But Jesus shatters all previous ideas by claiming that the bread which he was about to give them was not Wisdom, but his flesh. Even more outrageously, he claimed that this bread was not just for the people of the Law, but 'for the life of the world' (v. 51).

Little wonder that they argued over such an outrageous and obnoxious idea: a man who gives his flesh to eat (v. 52)! Jesus' answer to their puzzlement points beyond the immediate discussion. He speaks to them about eating the flesh and drinking the blood of the Son of Man

(v. 53). The Son of Man is the one who must be 'lifted up' on a Cross (see 3:13-14; 8:28; 12:32). It is only through the piercing and breaking apart of a body that flesh can be had and that blood will be spilt. So will it be with Jesus. There is only one true bread and drink which brings a life that ordinary food can never provide (vv. 55-56), and it comes from Jesus crucified.

Here we are at the heart of the mystery of the Eucharist. The Gospel urges us to look behind the rituals we celebrate as we gather around the altar. What is taking place in the eucharistic celebration is a dramatic recalling of a body broken and blood spilt, so that the love of God can be seen. Jesus not only talked about God; he showed God to us through his loving gift of himself. As he said: 'When I am lifted up on a Cross, then I will draw everyone to myself' (12:32). How right the Gospel writer was when he closed the account of the crucifixion of Jesus with the words: 'They shall gaze upon him whom they pierced' (19:37). In the Eucharist, we see love.

The life-giving power of the Eucharist does not come simply from the fact that we eat and drink. It comes from the challenging presence of a loving God, made available to us in a body broken and blood spilt, because of that love. When St Paul wrote to the Corinthians about their celebration of the Eucharist he reminded them: 'Until the Lord comes, therefore, you are proclaiming his death' (1 Cor 11:26). As Jesus shows his love for us in his body broken and his blood spilt, so we are asked to do the same. 'Go, the Mass has ended' means: Go now and do likewise because 'you are proclaiming the Lord's death'. Eucharist is not only an act of cultic worship; it is a way of life.

SECOND SUNDAY OF THE YEAR

John 1:29-34

Lamb of God — Son of God

In the Prologue to the Fourth Gospel (Jn 1:1-18) John the Baptist was presented to the reader of the Gospel as the one sent from God to bear witness to the Word (vv. 6-8). A God-sent witness can only tell the truth about Jesus. People from Jerusalem tried to force the Baptist into accepting messianic ideas which they entertained about him (1:19-28). His only answer to their probing was to say 'I am not' (see vv. 21-22). The next day, as Jesus comes towards him, the Baptist turns from his negative witness to point to Jesus as the Lamb of God who takes away the sin of the world (v. 29) and the Chosen One of God (v. 34).

The Baptist engaged in his baptising ministry in a profound obedience to the design of God. He did not 'know' everything that would be asked of him. He simply accepted that he was doing what God had called him to do: to reveal the coming one to Israel (vv. 30-31). The expression 'the one who comes after me' usually refers to a disciple of a master, but here the one who follows is greater than John the Baptist who goes before him (v. 30). As John was prepared to accept God's sent one, now he asks that an unknowing Israel might accept the revelation of God which Jesus will bring (v. 31).

The Baptist 'recalls' the events which only he has witnessed. The people he is speaking to *in* the story and we readers *of* the story were not at these events, and thus must accept his testimony. Jesus is the Lamb of God, the Chosen One of God, the one 'who baptises with the Holy

Spirit', forming a new people (vv. 32-34). At least the reader of the Gospel has read the Prologue and is aware that exalted claims have been made for the Word who became flesh in the person of Jesus Christ (see 1:14-17), but now the Baptist is enlarging on that information. The descent of the Spirit (v. 32) indicates that Jesus is not only 'the Christ', but he is the Lamb of God, the Chosen One of God.

The Lamb *of* God takes away the sins of the world because he is from God. It is as the Lamb *of* God that he takes away the sins of the world. Only God takes away, or forgives sins. Through the use of a sacrificed lamb, the people of Israel established and renewed their union with God and among themselves after sin. Jesus is now presented as the lamb, but he is not of the same order. He is not a 'cultic offering' taken from among us. Jesus is 'of God', given to us. The former rites of a sacrificed lamb, so important to the history, faith and culture of the People of God have been transcended. God now gives the fulness of pardon to Israel and to the whole world through the Lamb of God who takes away the sins of the world. Jesus is the one through whom God enters the human story, his Chosen One, offering it perfect reconciliation with him.

This new way to establish union between ourselves and our God has been made possible because the Lamb of God is the Chosen One of God. In Jesus of Nazareth, heaven and earth meet. The union between ourselves and the union with our God has been perfected in the gift of Jesus. This is an incredible claim, something we so often take for granted. There is need for wonder and delight at what God has done for us, leading to a grateful raising of our hearts and minds in prayer, in recognition of the gift of Jesus. One from among us has taken away the sins of the world, enabling us to become children of God (see 1:13).

THIRD SUNDAY OF THE YEAR

Matthew 4:12-23

The good news of the kingdom

The Gospel of Matthew is introduced by a lengthy 'prologue' (Mt 1:1-4:11) which tells of Jesus' infancy (chs 1-2), the preaching of John the Baptist (3:1-12), the baptism of Jesus, and which concludes with a voice from heaven announcing: 'This is my Son' (3:13-17). Jesus' sonship is then immediately 'tested' by the devil, but the devil is vanquished: 'The devil left him, and angels appeared and looked after him' (4:1-11). The stage is now set for the public ministry of Jesus, and the story begins with today's Gospel reading (4:12-23).

The precursor has been taken away with his arrest (v. 12), and Jesus settles in the lakeside town of Capernaum. The geographical location of Capernaum summons from the Evangelist the memory of a prophecy from Isaiah: from the way of the sea, from Galilee of the nations will go forth a great light (see Is 8:23-9:1). Galilee is not only the northern section of the land of Israel. It has been and will further prove to be 'Galilee of the nations', the origin of Good News for the whole world. From the first moments of Jesus' ministry his mission to the whole world, to 'the nations', is announced.

The first words of the ministry of Jesus call for all to turn back from their present way of living into a new way of relating to God. Jesus has come to bring the Good News: God's kingdom is breaking into the human story. We are summoned to conversion that we may be part of the reigning presence of God. But Jesus does not only tell us that God's reign has broken into the human story in his person. He shows the power of this kingdom in the calling of the first disciples.

Jesus journeys on relentlessly, responding to his own God-given mission: 'As he was walking by the Sea of Galilee' (v. 18); 'Going on from there' (v. 21). While on this journey, he sees (v. 18), he speaks (v. 19), he calls (v. 21). He summons these fishermen away from all the things regarded by their peer group as the signs of their success: their nets, their boats and their Father. The initiative lies entirely with him: 'I will make you fishers of men' (v. 19). The disciple is called to the 'following' of Jesus, going down the same way, joining Jesus on his journey, never leading, never dictating terms in the kingdom. Without a word, they followed him (vv. 20, 22).

The Evangelist Matthew has drawn a portrait of the way the Lord breaks into the life of his disciple. But as our own experience of discipleship teaches us, our response does not always match the ideals portrayed here. The Evangelist deliberately idealises the vocation of the first disciples to show that Jesus' presence has already set into motion God's reigning presence among us. God's kingdom is present when disciples respond unquestioningly to the mystery of God's ways.

It is not only in the story of human beings that God exercises his kingship. The powers of sickness and evil can never be victorious against it. Indeed, wherever Jesus went proclaiming the Kingdom, its presence was immediately obvious (v. 23). All kinds of disease and sickness simply cease before the power of God's goodness. Perhaps the absence of God's presence as King among us and the presence of so much sickness and evil is in some way linked with the ambiguity of our response to his summons to follow Jesus.

FOURTH SUNDAY OF THE YEAR

Matthew 5:1-12

A program for blessedness

The ministry of Jesus is now under way. He has proclaimed the coming of the Kingdom, called his first followers, and overcome the evils of sickness and demon possession (Mt 4:12-25). Strangely, this feverish activity of the first day of Jesus at Capernaum ceases abruptly as 'seeing the crowds, he went up the hill. There he sat down and was joined by his disciples. Then he began to speak' (5:1-2). The original Greek tells us that Jesus went up on to 'the mountain', rather than 'up the hill'.

At Jesus' birth innocent male children were slain, just as at Moses' birth innocent male children were slain (Mt 2:16-18; Ex 1:15-22). Just as Moses came out of Egypt, leading the people of God into their Land, so also it is said of Jesus 'I called my son out of Egypt' (2:15, citing Hos 11:1). As once the Law was given to Moses on the mountain of Sinai (Ex 19:16-20:17), now the new and perfect Moses, Jesus, gathers a new people of God, his disciples, on a mountain, a New Sinai, to give them a New Law. The beatitudes (5:1-12) open a long discourse, commonly called 'the sermon on the mount' which is a program for the Christian life (5:1-7:28).

Jesus tells his disciples that they have been blessed (our Lectionary's 'happy' is a weak rendering of the Greek word) in a particular way if their lives have certain qualities. To be gentle, to mourn, to thirst for what is right, to be merciful, pure in heart and a peacemaker are the signs of the presence of the kingdom of God in our lives. To have such virtues is a sign of blessedness; a sign that

God has done something for you. We do not acquire these qualities simply by our own will-power and hard work. We receive them from a loving God, if we abandon our own attempts to impose our agendas, and accept his way.

This is the reason for our happiness: God gifts us with the virtues that proclaim his presence in our lives. There are four qualities in the Christian life which show our *receptivity* to the goodness of God: poverty of spirit, gentleness, a preparedness to mourn and a hunger for justice. Then there are four further qualities which demonstrate our preparedness to *actively work* for the extension of God's kingdom: the gift of mercy, a single-minded commitment to the ways of God without any ambiguity (purity of heart is not about one's sexual situation . . . even though it follows from a commitment to the ways of God), a preparedness to create peace around us and a willingness to love the Lord, cost us what it may.

Jesus concludes by speaking to the experience of the Church. Although originally aimed at the early Church which first used this Gospel, the words which conclude the beatitudes are still urgently relevant: 'Happy are you when people abuse you and persecute you and speak all kinds of calumny against you' (v. 11). In the name of Jesus, we stand over against the arrogant secularism which has pushed Christianity to the peripheries of Western society and culture. Subtle forms of persecution and calumny are a part of our every-day experience. Let us face this joyfully and realistically. To live this situation reflecting the blessedness which flows from the gifts of God, merits the final gift of his never-ending presence to us: 'Rejoice and be glad, for your reward will be great' (v. 12).

FIFTH SUNDAY OF THE YEAR

Matthew 5:13-16

To be salt and light

One of the problems which may emerge from a Christian life which depends only upon the beatitudes of last week's Gospel (Mt 5:1-12) is that the Christian life becomes a contented peacefulness. With the gifts of God we are able to face happily the difficulties of life. Jesus' teaching of the beatitudes should have this effect upon us, but there is a risk that it might produce only that.

To avoid this risk, immediately after the beatitudes Jesus tells three very short parables about salt, a city high on a hill and a lamp. Having told his disciples of their giftedness, he now teaches them about the task of the people of God in the world. They have received God's good gifts; they must now bear the fruits of their giftedness.

The old Law was regarded as the salt which gave taste to Jewish life. Jesus now tells his followers they have been specially gifted (last week's Gospel) so that they go beyond the ways of the Law. As Matthew's readers knew from their former life within Judaism, there was always a danger that people might simply live an external observance of the Law. To live in that way takes God's gifts for granted, and the vivifying salt loses its taste. Its enriching flavour can never be restored. If this could happen with Israel where an observance of the Law became a heartless ritual, so can it also be with the Christian who is challenged to give flavour to the world. The Law gave life to Israel; the Christian is able to give life to the world. But what of Christians who take their giftedness for granted? They, like tasteless salt, are only fit to be 'thrown out and trampled underfoot' (v. 13).

As the Law of Israel should have been salt to the nation, so also was it the light of the nation. Jesus again uses a metaphor applied to the Law to speak to his disciples. They are not the light of a nation; they are 'the light of the world' (v. 14). The links with the past experience of the early Christian Church continue as Jesus speaks of 'a city built on a hill-top' which cannot be hidden. The reference is to Jerusalem, the Holy City where God dwelt in his Temple. It could not be hidden, and it was only fitting that it stood before all as a witness of God's presence to his people. So should it also be with the Christian.

Lights are to give light, not to be hidden under any form of container which would eliminate the rays of light (v. 15). The Christian life can give light to a world looking for direction and purpose. The good life of the followers of Jesus leads genuine searchers to look beyond the individual Christian to the God who graces certain human beings. In this way they too 'give the praise to your Father in heaven' (v. 16).

Jesus' disciples are to be salt of the earth and light for humankind. The obvious quality of their lives, not the following of an external law, will mark their discipleship. The Law, the former salt and light, will be perfected if Christians are prepared to be salt of the earth and light to the world. This does not call for extraordinary measures . . . just good Christian lives. In this way others will be attracted to the city on the hill, and they too will give praise to our Father in heaven.

SIXTH SUNDAY OF THE YEAR

Matthew 5:17-37

The perfection of the Law

Last week's Gospel shifted the symbols of salt and light away from the Law in Israel to the Christian in the world (Mt 5:13-16). How did Jesus relate to the Law? Was its place in God's saving purpose finished? Today's Gospel focuses its attention upon these questions.

Jesus did not come to abolish the Law, but he claims that he has come to bring it to perfection (v. 17). There is a way in which the Law must be lived for it really to be the Law of God. Jesus will not only tell his disciples that they must live the perfection of the Law, but he shows them such a life-style. Jesus himself will be the embodiment of the perfection of the Law.

Today's Gospel reading is one of the key passages for a proper understanding of the Gospel of Matthew. Until such time as the law is perfected, when heaven and earth pass away, every detail of the Law must be lived. Jesus tells his disciples that 'till heaven and earth disappear . . . until its purpose is achieved' (v. 18). Notice the double use of words which indicate a future time: 'till . . . until'. When might that time be?

One might think that these references to a future time point to the traditional idea of the final end of all time; but this is not the case for Matthew. It is not at the end of the world, but at the end of Jesus' life. When he comes to his death, the skies darken, there is an earthquake and the rocks split. The holy ones of old rise from their tombs and are seen in the city (see 27:51-54). At his resurrection, the guards are struck down as if dead, angels appear in blinding light, and there is a further earthquake (see 28:2-4). Heaven and earth are passing away! The life, death and resurrection of Jesus mark the time when the Law is brought to its perfection.

How does the follower of Jesus share in his perfect living of the Law? Jesus moves steadily through the old Law given to Moses at Sinai: 'You have learnt how it was said to our ancestors . . .' (vv. 21, 27, 31, 33). This is a stock phrase which a Jewish reader immediately recognises as a reference to the Law given to Moses at Sinai. But each of these ancient and sacred Laws is reinterpreted on the basis of the authority of the person and the word of Jesus himself: 'But I say this to you . . .' (vv. 22, 28, 32, 34). Another 'stock phrase' has been introduced. God's ways are now being further explained by the words of Jesus: 'I say this to you'.

However, the Laws given of old are not denied. Jesus does not quote the laws against killing, adultery and divorce only to deny them. He does not exhort his followers to contradict such laws by killing, committing adultery and divorcing. On the contrary. Much of *what we must do* has not changed, but *why we do it* has.

Jesus calls his followers to a righteousness which arises from a deeply felt Christian commitment to his life-style. The key to today's Gospel is found in a modern paraphrase of the words of Jesus: 'For I tell you, if your virtue goes no deeper than that of those who only behave in a certain way because they feel they have to, you will never get into the kingdom of heaven' (see v. 20).

SEVENTH SUNDAY OF THE YEAR

Matthew 5:38-48

To be perfect as our Father is perfect

The pattern of Jesus' teaching continues. Jesus quotes from the Law given on the former mountain of Sinai: 'You have learnt how it was said . . .' (vv. 38, 43), counterbalanced by the new law, given on another mountain, which has its origin and its meaning in the word and person of Jesus himself: 'But I say this to you . . .' (vv. 39, 44). Jesus calls Christians not only to righteousness according to the Law, but to a higher righteousness based upon a commitment to his word and person.

But, unlike the earlier part of Jesus' sermon, here principles which stood behind the former Law call for more radical reform. He now points to an aspect of the Law which cannot be part of Christianity. The Law permitted an eye for an eye and a tooth for a tooth, and the love of neighbour but hatred of enemy. These seemingly harsh laws made sense in the lives of a nomadic people, struggling for existence in a hostile world.

The law concerning an eye for an eye and a tooth for a tooth was a limitation upon the vendettas which inevitably took place within the community. The law on love of neighbour and hatred of enemy made sure that the community protected itself against its enemies. A small wandering people defended itself and its future by such laws. But the new Law of Jesus teaches that such considerations are now transcended by the universal vocation to love which has been unleashed upon the world in the life, death and resurrection of Jesus of Nazareth.

How often it is said that the basic law of Christianity is the law of love, but how little that is genuinely practised. What marks our so-called Christian world today: vendetta and self protection, or universal love and forgiveness? It must be honestly admitted that while many professing Christians today have a firm belief in God, they have lost serious interest in following Jesus. In the increasingly competitive world, the most important thing is one's own professional and financial security and progress. There is little place in today's world for such attitudes as: 'If anyone hits you on the right cheek, offer him the other as well' (v. 39), or 'Give to anyone who asks, and if anyone wants to borrow, do not turn away' (v. 42).

One might even ask: what marks the Christian Churches of today: vendetta and self protection, or universal love? God may well be in place, but what of Jesus and his teaching? We will all have our own experience to look back to in our answer to those questions, but ultimately they all come home: what marks my Christian life: self-protection or universal love. Even in our practice of Christianity are we not too interested in 'What's in it for me?'.

The quality of our love is no small matter. It is the measure of our godliness. We all sense our capacity to love and to be loved, 'the desire to be desired by the one we desire'. It is in this that we sense the presence of the divine within us. In Jesus' command to perfect love he is teaching us the way to be the signs and bearers of God's love in the world. It is not as if we somehow represent God . . . we are his very presence. In loving as Jesus loved we become perfect as our heavenly Father is perfect (v. 48).

EIGHTH SUNDAY OF THE YEAR

Matthew 6:24-34

The Master of our tomorrows

Profound truths can be expressed in simple proverbs because they arise from a genuine experience of the most important things in life. Today's Gospel begins with one of those proverbs which may well have been in use at the time of Jesus. Arising out of his own experience of the human situation, Jesus has recourse to a proverb: 'No one can be the slave of two masters' (Mt 6:24). No matter what one's religious persuasions might be, this affirmation is true. One's heart and service can only be given to one Master. In any situation of divided loyalties the human heart is so made that one will suffer, as the other is pursued.

Having made this more general point, Jesus teaches what he means through a series of two very beautiful images: the birds in the sky, the flowers growing in the fields (vv. 26-30). Birds 'do not sow or reap', but God feeds them (v. 26). Flowers, more beautifully arrayed than 'Solomon in all his regalia' (v. 30) neither work nor spin but are clothed by God.

The undeniable beauty of the birds of the air and the flowers of the fields flows from their total dependence upon God. Jesus' sensitivity to the beautiful things of this world was very much a part of his life-style, but he did not stop at a simple admiration of the world. He was moved by them, but he looked beyond and through them, to see the creative and caring presence of God, whom he called Father, and whom he taught us to call Father (see also Mt 6:9-13). Jesus believed passionately that this is where human beings will find beauty and peace.

Yet so much of our lives, especially in our modern Western society marked by extremes of both affluence and poverty, is directed by the questions: What are we to eat? What are we to drink? How are we to be clothed? (see v. 31). Most of us spend our todays worrying about and organising our tomorrows, and most of our tomorrows trying to sort out the mess because things did not turn out the way we had planned yesterday! Of course, we have a responsibility to act creatively and caringly in the world which God the creator gives into our hands. But it is ultimately God who is the Master of our tomorrow.

This is an important principle for the Christian life. There comes a time in everybody's story when there are no more tomorrows. It is a strange thing that the everyday encounters which we have with the reality of death, and even the dramatic experience of the death of our loved ones seldom teaches us that we cannot ultimately determine our future. Yet, as Christians, we confess that at the moment of death we fall into the merciful and loving hands of our God. Then we will know that he is the Master of our tomorrows.

But why wait for death to learn this lesson? In the midst of our many and necessary concerns we must develop a trust in that good God who is the ultimate end of all our history. God is the great and good creator of our Bible and Christian tradition; God is the Master of our tomorrows. Our tomorrows will be much better left in his hands than anything we can arrange. Tomorrow will take care of itself. Each day has enough trouble of its own (see v. 34).

NINTH SUNDAY OF THE YEAR

Matthew 7:21-27

Those who say 'Lord, Lord'

Earlier in the Sermon on the Mount, Jesus taught his disciples to pray (see Mt 6:9-13). He taught them to relate to God as Father, to ask that his will be done always and that his kingdom come. Today's Gospel is closely linked with that prayer. It is the more practical side of the medal, because prayer is not only about the words we say, but also about the lives we lead.

It is possible for words to become cheap. Jesus was particularly hard on any form of false religion. He related to the God of Israel as his Son, but he was unhappy with any form of Jewish religion which did not put its life where its words were. The Gospels are full of such episodes, none more pointed than the parable of the Pharisee and the Publican (see Lk 18:9-14). It is not enough to say the words 'Lord, Lord'. That is easy. Entry into the kingdom which Jesus has brought into our story will only come by relating to God as any true daughter or son relates to a parent: they do the will of God (v. 21).

There have always been people who appear to be religious because they are 'proper'. They say the expected things at the right time, and they behave in an acceptable way. But where are their hearts? They are warned by Jesus that the falseness of their acclaim from the world will one day be called into question. It is not the fine words, the casting out of demons or the working of miracles that will bring final union with God. Indeed, many who lay claim to such performances will be told: 'Away from me, you evil men' (vv. 22-23).

What, then, is asked of the true believer? Jesus tells us that 'everyone who listens to these words of mine and acts on them will be like a sensible man who built his house on rock' (v. 24). Jesus' demand that we 'listen to these words' is not some generic request about his overall teaching. 'These words' apply specifically to his attack on people who say the right things and perform the right way, but who do it for their own public image or because it fits their own agenda (see vv. 21-23). Grandeur built up in this way — and there is a great deal of such grandeur in the Christian Churches — will collapse like a house built on sand (see v. 26). As always with the unexpected: 'what a fall it had!' (v. 27).

One of the difficulties the Christian Church faces is the criticism levelled against it that its practising members are Sunday Christians and week-day pagans. So many of us do the 'proper thing' for our Sunday liturgy, but fail to repeat the challenge of the Eucharist in our daily living. It is urgent that we who claim to be Christians, who say 'Lord, Lord', listen to the word of Jesus and act upon it (v. 24).

Many today have their self-centred agenda and leave the practice of their faith claiming that belief in Jesus has nothing to do with 'going to Mass on Sunday'. We live in what is sometimes called the post-Christian age. Why do we persist? We 'go to Mass on Sunday' because we believe that sharing in the word of Jesus and responding to the challenge of the 'memorial' of his love for us makes sense out of everything that we do and say; not only on Sunday, but always and everywhere.

TENTH SUNDAY OF THE YEAR

Matthew 9:9-13

What I want is mercy

Many features in the story of the call of Matthew, the tax-collector, repeat the earlier call of the first four disciples (see Mt 4:18-22). Jesus calls others away from their normal situation in life, and asks them to join him in his journey: 'Follow me'. Reflecting the ideal response to the call of Jesus, we read that Matthew never hesitates. Not a word to ask who Jesus is, or what he might expect of his followers: Matthew 'got up and followed him' (v. 9).

The call of Matthew, however, does not simply repeat the call of the first four disciples. The point is been made that Matthew was 'sitting by the customs house' and that he is a tax collector (see also 10:3). Such people lived on the fringes of Jewish society. Working to gather taxes for a foreign power, they had sold their birthright to make profit from the presence of a non-Jewish government in God's land. This, of course, was the most serious reason for hatred. However, they were also well known as people who overtaxed, to create a comfortable margin between what they had to pay, and what they could keep as personal profit.

Jesus has called a sinner who, because of his sin, had become an outcast, to be one of his followers. This links the call of Matthew to the passage which follows. Jesus has not only called a tax-collector to be a disciple, but he sits at table with more tax collectors and a further group of people called 'sinners' (v. 10). This generic term was applied to social outcasts, people made unclean through their breaking of certain laws or their following a disreputable profession. Sitting at table with these people indicated Jesus' preparedness to share life and fellowship with them.

In strictly religious terms, the Pharisees are right in questioning Jesus' disciples about this practice (v. 11). How could Jesus possibly be a holy man, or a religious leader of any significance? Jesus' answer informs them that he has come to fulfil the plans of God, not the expectations of accepted religious authorities. This is shown through the use of Scripture. Anything said by one of the Prophets indicated God's design. Hosea had announced, in the name of YHWH: 'What I want is mercy, not sacrifice' (Hos 6:6. See Mt 9:13).

There are many people in society who need the help of God, the help of their fellow-human beings and, ultimately, salvation. Jesus has come for these people; he has come for the sick (v. 12) for the sinners (v. 13). The healthy and the virtuous have no need for help and salvation. This is a subtle attack on the Pharisees, who regarded themselves as 'healthy' and 'virtuous' — but were they? Was there no place for the merciful presence of God among them?

The situation has not changed a great deal over the centuries. We Christians (today's Pharisees?) sometimes appear to belong to a rather exclusive club, where the good people belong and where the sinners are to be excluded. Do I not have a tendency to look down upon the 'sick' and the 'sinners'? Today's Gospel urges us to recall God's design: 'What I want is mercy, not sacrifice'. Christians and the Christian Churches must accept the challenge to show the world the face of mercy, not judgment and condemnation.

ELEVENTH SUNDAY OF THE YEAR

Matthew 9:36—10:8

To be missionaries of Jesus

Thus far Matthew's story of Jesus has been marked by Jesus' missionary activity. As he began his ministry the narrator commented: 'He went around the whole of Galilee, teaching in their synagogues, proclaiming the Good News of the Kingdom and curing all kinds of diseases and sickness among the people' (Mt 4:23). At the close of a series of miracles (chs 8-9) the narrator repeats that Jesus was 'teaching in their synagogues, proclaiming the Good News of the Kingdom and curing all kinds of diseases and sickness (9:35).

The foundation for the Christian mission has been laid in the missionary activity of Jesus himself. Now he associates the followers he has chosen to join his mission. Seeing the plight of the people, like sheep without a shepherd (v. 36), he asks his disciples to pray for workers in the harvest (v. 37). However, they are not only to pray for workers in the harvest, they are commissioned to be workers in the harvest (10:1-8). Notice how carefully their commission repeats what has already been said of Jesus. He had cast out demons and cured all kinds of diseases and sickness (see 4:23; 9:35). Now they are given authority to do the same (10:1). They are to repeat what Jesus had done; they are to spread the missionary activity of Jesus.

The list of names has its importance. Simon, first in the list, is given a further name: 'Peter' (10:2). The expression 'peter' in Greek or Aramaic was never used as a person's name. It was a word meaning 'rock'. The reader wonders what this word now used as a person's name might mean, but that story will be told later in the Gospel (see 16:18-20). The last name, Judas, is further qualified: 'the one who was to betray him' (10:4). The list begins with a figure who will eventually be the rock upon which the Church is built, and ends with another figure who will betray Jesus. Both, however, are disciples and missionaries of Jesus.

For the moment fragile disciples are sent out to bring the message of the Kingdom of God only to the lost sheep of Israel (vv. 5-7). Later the commission will become universal (see 28:16-20). In the overall structure of Matthew's story of Jesus this present limitation links them more closely to Jesus' mission. During his ministry, he too goes only to the lost sheep of the house of Israel (see 15:24). After the paschal mystery the message will be preached to all the nations (see 20:19). Disciples are to repeat the mission of Jesus (v. 8), but only because they depend entirely upon him. They are his disciples; they are not masters. They were called by him, they received without charge; now they are to give what they have received and learnt from him without charge.

The mission of Jesus continues. We are called to repeat what Jesus did, to bring peace and healing to all who are sick, and all who are troubled. The Kingdom of God is at hand. However, in our fragility we must recognise that we are capable of being both Peter the Rock and Judas the betrayer. We are no better than the next person. What we are given and learn from our Christian lives and experience is a gift. It is not a gift, however, to be jealously guarded within the exclusive club of the Christian Church. It has been given to us without charge. We must give without charge.

TWELFTH SUNDAY OF THE YEAR

Matthew 10:26-33

Fearlessness

Last week's Gospel introduced the disciples to the mission of Jesus. Today's reading continues the same theme. During the course of his missioning speech to his disciples, Jesus three times tells them: 'Do not be afraid' (Mt 10:26, 28, 31). This indicates that the Christian message created opposition from its very beginnings. The life-story of Jesus, which led to violent death, will always be present in the life-story of his Church, however we might try to hide it behind the pomp and triumphalism that sometimes mark the Church's external appearance.

Yet, no matter what the preachers of the Good News might suffer, the Gospel cannot be finally hidden (vv. 26-27). The constant exposure to physical risk and even death must not frighten disciples (v. 28). It calls for these words of encouragement from Jesus. To preach and to bear witness to the Good News of the Kingdom of God may not lead to physical suffering and persecution in the Western World, but it leads to the more subtle persecution of marginalisation. Such a message and way of life create ridicule in contemporary society, although the ridicule can sometimes be hollow, as that same society is unable to find solutions to its deepest crises.

The terrors of this world do concern us, but Jesus asks us to transcend anything that human beings can do to us. There is a greater danger: the threats of the evil one who can destroy persons by leading them into an eternal damnation (v. 28). Behind this traditional message stands a profound truth, central to Christian belief: what we do in this life brings joy and happiness not only in this life, but forever. There is a secure way of overcoming the fear of falling prey to the evil one: complete trust in the Father who lovingly watches over the life and death of even his smallest and least valuable creatures. This good Father watches over his children whom he knows and cares for, down to the smallest detail of their lives (vv. 29-31).

Armed with this confidence, the disciple must bear witness before hostile tribunals. The disciple who leans on a loving Father to gain courage to bear witness to his Son will one day receive loving testimony from that Son at the final tribunal. But Jesus will disown the weak and selfish disciple who does not stand by him (vv. 32-33). If the disciple is not prepared to be a sister or brother to Jesus — how can such a disciple claim to be a son or daughter of the Father of Jesus?

We are called to do the work of Jesus, however modest our role may be. This task will inevitably lead to difficulties, suffering and contradiction. The mysteries which we try to live will eventually be proclaimed as the final truths. Only one thing should strike fear: a sinfulness which comes from our inability to rest securely in the goodness and strength of God, our Father.

Sin is not so much the wicked things which somehow continue to emerge in our lives. We must all admit that too often we bring hurt into our lives and the lives of others; we sin. But sinfulness is a manifestation of our lack of trust in God. We act as if we were god to ourselves. But we sinners must not be afraid. God will have the last word, and Jesus will be there to present his sinful and saved brothers and sisters to his Father and our Father.

THIRTEENTH SUNDAY OF THE YEAR

Matthew 10:37-42

The cost and the rewards of discipleship

Jesus' missionary discourse began with his command to the disciples that they were to go only to the lost sheep of Israel (see Mt 10:6). Today's Gospel shows no limitations. The word which most frequently is used throughout Jesus' address to his disciples is 'anyone' (see vv. 37, 38, 39, 40, 41, 42). A part of Jesus' message is that racial and national concerns do not influence the following of Jesus. The kingdom which he has come to bring is not limited to Israel. The kingdom of God is available to 'anyone'.

The passage itself is carefully structured. First Jesus tells of three ways in which 'anyone' will be unworthy of discipleship (vv. 37-38). A further central affirmation on losing and finding life (v. 39), and, finally, three ways in which 'anyone' will be able to show himself or herself worthy of Jesus and the reward which he has come to bring (vv. 40-42).

Jesus does not mince matters. He is to be the centre, the focal-point of the life of 'anyone' who would claim to be his follower. To make this clear he choses the family, the place seen in all cultures as having a prior place in our hearts, calling for our care and attention. However, not even the bonds which tie child to father or mother (v. 37) or parent to child (v. 38) must be allowed to come before one's attachment to Jesus.

This does not mean that the bonds between parents and children are to be in any way lessened in importance in the Christian world. Indeed, the command to love must be lived in the home. However, great as the bonds of true family affection may be, the bond which unites the Christian to Jesus must be greater. Jesus uses this approach, not to play down our love for one another, but to show just how significant must be the bond between Jesus and his followers. Such close attachment to a man who went to a Cross will be difficult. It will summon from us a loving gift of ourselves, so that others may have life. We must be prepared to take up the Cross, as he took up his (vv. 38-39). But strangely, the loss of self in love does not lead to misery. Our own experience tells us that such a life-style produces lasting love and joy in this life. Jesus adds to this by telling us that it will produce eternal love and joy (v. 39).

The positive signs of a disciple of Jesus make this clear; welcoming, allowing other people, with all their needs, to come into our lives. In welcoming the prophet or the holy man (v. 41), in offering respite and hospitality to the person in need, even by so small a gesture as a cup of cold water (v. 42), we welcome Jesus himself (v. 40). It is the way we place others before ourselves, caring for them in the little and large things, that we welcome Jesus who is always among us in his people. But Jesus does not come alone. In welcoming Jesus, we welcome the one who sent him.

The way we deal with others is the measure of the presence of God in our lives. The joy this brings is ours to be had now — but the word of Jesus also tells us that to welcome people in this way is a sure way to an everlasting reward (v. 42).

FOURTEENTH SUNDAY OF THE YEAR

Matthew 11:25-30

Taking on the burden

So much is said about Jesus. He works miracles (Mt 8-9) and he commissions his disciples to follow him in his mission (ch 10). Jesus is to be the focal point for the life of the disciple (10:37-42). The way of telling the story could lead the reader of the Gospel to lose sight of the centrality of God in the Christian life: 'the one who sent' Jesus (see 10:40). This danger is averted in today's Gospel, as Jesus points away from himself towards his Father. Everything Jesus says and does comes from his Father: 'Everything has been entrusted to me by my Father' (11:26). The learned and the clever are unable to reach beyond what they see happening before their eyes. They do not even wonder about the more profound mystery of the God and Father of Jesus who sent him (v. 25).

Some, however, do not need to be able to control all the answers with their own schemes. These are the ones who are not full of themselves and their own abilities and achievements. The image of 'mere children' is carefully chosen (v. 25). To be a child does not mean to be ignorant or irresponsible. It means to adopt that receptive attitude of a child to whom everything is new. Children wait, with an open mind and an open heart, to receive all the wonderful new things that happen and are said each day. They have space in their hearts, their minds and their lives to receive the gifts which are given to them. Thus it is with true followers of Jesus. They too have space in their hearts, their minds and their lives to receive the gifts the Father gives them. The greatest of all these gifts is his Son.

In today's Gospel Jesus expresses one of the main beliefs of the Christian Faith. The Father of Jesus would be unknown, were it not for Jesus his Son. Jesus knows the Father, and makes him known to us (v. 27). Without Jesus, the deepest longings of all women and men would not have their ultimate answer: the God and Father of Jesus who is also our God and Father. The Gospel of John says this so clearly: 'No one has ever seen God. His only begotten Son, who is turned in loving union towards his Father, he has told his story' (Jn 1:18). By means of his life, teaching, death and resurrection, by means of his 'story', Jesus has made the unseen God known to us. Have we made space to receive that knowledge?

In the time of Jesus it was thought that one could only know God by the exact observance of the yoke and burden of the Law. There were 613 laws which, if perfectly lived, assured the faithful Israelite of a righteousness in the eyes of God. Jesus does not take away the obligations of law. After all, he did not come to destroy the Law and the Prophets, he came to bring them to perfection (see 5:17). But Jesus offers a new yoke and a new burden (v. 29).

The words of Jesus must be taken seriously. A yoke and a burden there must be in Christianity. There is a discipline to the Christian life. We must be prepared to take on the command of Jesus to love, and we must try to live the Gospel we proclaim. That can, at times, appear to be a yoke and a burden, but Jesus assures us that it frees our hearts and responds to our deepest needs. That is why it is easy and light; that is why in taking the risk of opening ourselves and accepting the God and Father of Jesus as our God and Father we will find rest for our souls.

FIFTEENTH SUNDAY OF THE YEAR

Matthew 13:1-23

A seed is sown and will bear fruit

From a makeshift pulpit off the shore, Jesus teaches one of his most famous parables: the parable of the Sower. In Jesus' world there were no fences, no machines and no carefully designed fields. The sower did not first plough the field and then carefully sow seed into a ploughed ground. The first thing to be done was to sow the seed, casting it widely and almost indiscriminately while walking (Mt 13:4-5). Once the seed had been cast, the land was ploughed. In these conditions, seed would be found in many places, but no matter where the seed fell, inevitably a crop would grow. However uneven the yield of the crop (vv. 5-9), it would be a fruitful crop, a hundredfold, sixty or thirty (v. 8).

The disciples are puzzled by Jesus' teaching in parables, as they demand a deeper understanding of the mystery behind them which most cannot grasp. Jesus' imperative: 'Listen, anyone who has ears' (v. 9), tells them this is important, but what does it mean? Jesus' words to the puzzled disciples mark a crucial stage in the development of Matthew's story. Jesus tells his disciples they have been given a privilege, as the secrets of the kingdom have been revealed to them. But there are some who have not been given this gift. Indeed, Jesus is punishing this world by speaking in a way that excludes them: 'The reason I talk to them in parables is that they look without seeing and listen without hearing or understanding' (v. 13).

The listeners are like the soil receiving the seed. Jesus' teaching hardens the hearts of some, and thus they remain in their ignorance. There are some, specially blessed, into whose hearts, minds and lives the seed sinks. Many have longed for such a gift, but it has been given only to those whom God has chosen (v. 17). For Matthew's story of Jesus, this moment marks Jesus' break with official Judaism, and from now on the hostility between Jesus and the children of Israel will increase. Their hearts are hardened, and they will refuse all that Jesus has come to make known (vv. 14-15).

After this discussion indicating the two worlds, those blessed by the kingdom and those who are not, there is a further explanation of the parable (vv. 18-23). Although the parable itself stresses that no matter where the seed falls, there will always be a full crop, the explanation of the parable takes a different direction. It concentrates on how one should receive the word. Some receive and some do not receive the word. How can this be?

The word of God comes to us through preaching, through the challenge to live good lives in a secular world, through the call to love selflessly in our families and in many other ways. How do we receive it? Could it be said of us that the word never lasts because it does not take root in us? Does the lure of the more attractive but ultimately vain things of this life choke the challenge of the word so that we produce nothing (vv. 21-22)? Of one thing we can be sure, whatever side we may take, in the end the seed of the word will produce fruit. Our Gospel today challenges us to see how privileged we are to hear the word. But that is only part of the story. We are also asked to consider how well and lastingly we receive it.

SIXTEENTH SUNDAY OF THE YEAR

Matthew 13:24-43

A mixed bag

Jesus' enigmatic way of teaching his disciples through parables continues. Closely linked to the parable of the sower follows a series of parables — still concerned with the sowing of seed. We hear of a man who sowed good seed but his enemy sowed darnel in his field (Mt 13:24-30); the smallest of the seed becomes a great tree (vv. 31-32); a tiny quantity of yeast leavens a batch of bread (v. 33).

Parallelling the parable of the sower, Jesus pauses for a moment to explain why he teaches through the use of parables (vv. 34-35). He then proceeds to explain the meaning of the parable of the darnel to his disciples (vv. 36-43). One of the attested truths about Jesus is that he taught through parables. In fact, this was Jesus' best way to teach the mysteries his Father entrusted to him.

It is not easy to 'expound things hidden since the foundation of the world' (v. 35). There are no words invented by human culture and history to speak of the mystery of God. The best place to look for such explanation is the reflected glory of God found in his creation. Thus Jesus points to the world about him, to the experience of being in the real world of day-to-day events so that he might tell stories which both catch the imagination of the listeners and lead them closer to understanding the one who sent him.

As Jesus went his way, preaching and making people whole, there was also a growing opposition to him. Many of his listeners knew that the powerful people in the land did not agree with him, and some may even have been aware that they were plotting his death. Within that setting Jesus tells them that he may appear weak and insignificant over against the great powers of this world. They should not fear. As with the smallest seed and the leaven, the kingdom Jesus preaches will not be brushed away (vv. 31-33). Indeed, while the powers of ancient Rome and ancient Israel have passed, we are privileged to be part of the gradual spread of the kingdom of Jesus' God and Father.

But both crops — good seed and darnel — are to grow together. Only at the final gathering is the separation to be made (vv. 29-30). It is in a real world that we must live. It is in a world tainted by sin, as well as institutionalised evil. The abuse of power, the enslavement and exploitation of the underprivileged and the slaying of the innocent have always been part of the human story. Are we able to grow strongly and mature well in the midst of all this darnel?

The key to the mystery of the mixed bag is confidence that the Lord of all history will be present when the crop is gathered (vv. 36-43). The parables which tell of an inevitable growth from something small and insignificant, be it a mustard seed or yeast in three measures of flour, encourage Christians who wonder why we always seem to be on the periphery. As the secular world takes a tighter grip on the way people think and act, we might wonder if there is still space for the kingdom of God. We must not fear. Jesus himself tells us to go on growing confidently in the midst of human ambiguity, trusting that it is our God who will finally reap an abundant crop, 'shining like the sun in the kingdom of the Father', despite the smallness of our external appearance (v. 43).

SEVENTEENTH SUNDAY OF THE YEAR

Matthew 13:44-52

The treasure of the kingdom

In order to teach as Jesus taught, the Church has placed most of Matthew's chapter on parables in the Lectionary. We have moved from Jesus' message on the inevitable victory of the kingdom of God (15th Sunday) to his teaching for us to recognise that the Christian life must be lived within of its own ambiguity and the ambiguity of the world (16th Sunday). Now Jesus focuses his attention more immediately upon the wonder of that kingdom.

Would it not be wonderful to find a great treasure in a field! How quickly we would sell everything we owned so to take possession of that field (v. 44). Similarly with the discovery of a unique pearl. How quickly we would let go of everything else we might treasure to have that one pearl (vv. 45-46).

But Jesus is not teaching us that the kingdom is a treasure or a pearl. That would be to miss the point by identifying the kingdom with a richness of this world. Nothing in this world matches the richness of the kingdom of God. Indeed, Jesus has to resort to an expression which opens up a distance between God's kingdom and the wonders of this world: 'The kingdom of God is like'. The kingdom is not 'the same as' anything in this world. The kingdom is worth the price of everything we have. To be part of the kingdom Jesus has come to establish among us we must be prepared to pay no less a price than everything. If we would sacrifice all that we have for a treasure hidden in a field or a pearl discovered by a merchant, what should we do for the kingdom?

It would be wonderful if we did judge the world in the light of the kingdom, so that even the most treasured things of this world would pale into insignificance before it. But, sadly, we all recognise that such is not the case. Thus, Jesus immediately adds another simile, comparing the kingdom to a dragnet which contains many types of fish (vv. 47-50). Like the parable of the darnel, which must be allowed to grow side by side with the good grain, the kingdom is likened to a net containing a haul of many kinds. Many of us may not be able to pay the price of everything. Yet we are part of that mixed bag, that net with many kinds. We must be happy to continue in the midst of our own ambiguity and the ambiguity of the Church and the people with whom and for whom we live. Let us leave to a good God and Father to make the final judgment (vv. 49-50).

In the meantime, Jesus poses a serious question — not only to his disciples in the Gospel, but also to disciples in the Church today. He asks: 'Have you understood all this?' (v. 51). With the disciples, we answer 'yes' to the question of Jesus. As we 'understand' the words which Jesus has spoken to us we attempt to live lives reflecting these words.

Living the parables of Jesus will be to go draw from our tradition, yet adapting it to the world we live in. It is thought that Matthew speaks of himself as a scribe who becomes a disciple in the kingdom of heaven (v. 52). He may have been a cultured Israelite who entered the Christian Church and wrote a Gospel which blends both old and new. But he is not the only one who became a disciple of the kingdom. We too are asked to bring out of our storeroom things both new and old (v. 52)

EIGHTEENTH SUNDAY OF THE YEAR

Matthew 14:13-21

You give them something to eat

With the death of the Baptist Jesus crosses the lake, to be alone with his disciples. But the people seek him out (Mt 14:13). The three characters of the story of the multiplication of the loaves and fishes have been introduced. The crowds travel the long distance around the lake to receive the wholeness which Jesus brought into their lives: 'As he stepped ashore he saw a large crowd; and he took pity on them and healed their sick' (v. 14). He is moved by the sight of their brokenness.

Now the crowds must be nourished for their journey. The disciples do not see this as their responsibility. They ask Jesus to send the people off to look after themselves: 'Send the people away and they can go to the villages to buy themselves some food' (v. 15). But people who have been restored to wholeness by Jesus must be nourished, and he demands that his disciples see to that nourishment: 'Give them something to eat yourselves' (v. 16). He has been unable to take the disciples into a lonely place to instruct them, but he will instruct them by calling them to minister to a broken and needy people.

The disciples can only reply in terms of the poverty of their possessions: 'All we have with us is five loaves and two fish' (v. 17). But Jesus asks them to come to him with the little they have. He accepts their poverty, blesses it and gives it back to them (v. 19). Jesus himself does not minister to the people; the disciples have the task of distributing the loaves to the crowd: 'He handed them to his disciples who gave them to the crowds' (v. 19). All are fed with as much as they want. Similarly, it is the disciples who gather the fragments into twelve baskets (v. 20). The large number of people — five thousand men, to say nothing of the women and children (v. 21) — add to the wonder of what has happened.

Reading this Gospel, we think immediately of the Eucharist. Jesus raises his eyes, blesses, breaks and the disciples distribute (v. 19). Jesus is the one who both restores the broken to wholeness (v. 14), and who nourishes them for the journey. It is not enough for Jesus to tell his people: 'Go, you have been healed'. He must also travel with them, nourishing them on their journey. However, it is not only Jesus who is involved in this task. He has intimately associated his disciples, and thus those of us who form the Church of today, with his life-giving mission. We are commanded to feed those in need.

Like the first disciples who preferred that the people go to the villages to look after themselves, we too shy clear of the challenge of Christian loving. This often happens because, again like the disciples in the story, we feel we have little or nothing to offer. But Jesus can take what little we have to offer, bless it, and give it back to us so that we might bring fulness to those whose lives we touch. As Jesus transforms the eucharistic bread, so he also transforms us into eucharistic people. The meal of Jesus is always open. The twelve baskets of fragments collected by the disciples indicate that the miraculous nourishment provided by Jesus is still available for those who seek it. As long as there are people looking for the gifts Jesus offers, this nourishment can never be totally consumed. But the story also tells us that Jesus wants disciples who are prepared to distribute his gifts.

NINETEENTH SUNDAY OF THE YEAR

Matthew 14:22-33

Little faith

Immediately after the miracle of the loaves and fishes, Jesus and the disciples are separated. The disciples are alone in the boat. Jesus is not with them, having remained behind to send away the crowds (v. 22). Two things are going on simultaneously. As the disciples set off across the lake, Jesus goes up on the mountain to pray (v. 23). The Lectionary says that he went 'into the hills', but this misses the biblical idea of Jesus ascending the mountain, a traditional place for contact with God. In prayer, Jesus returns to the source of all that he is and does.

But while Jesus is in close contact with God the crossing of the lake becomes a conflict, a battle with a heavy sea. The contrast between the situation of Jesus and that of his followers is vividly reported: 'When evening came he was there alone, while the boat, now far out on the lake, was battling with a heavy sea' (v. 24). Late in the night, Jesus comes to them out of the darkness, across the waters (v. 25). He has left the union of prayer with God to join his struggling disciples. Yet, despite their need for him, his presence strikes fear into their hearts as they cry out, 'It is a ghost' (v. 26).

Jesus reveals himself to them in a formula which has a long history in the Bible: 'It is I' (v. 27). From Moses' encounter with the burning bush (see Ex 3:14), down to the conflicts of the prophets with the false gods introduced into Israel (see especially Is 43:10; 45:18), this formula was used to speak of the presence of the true God to his people: 'It is I'. Over against all other gods, and all threats to his people, God is present to them. Equally important to moments when God or the Angel of God speaks to his people are the words of encouragement: 'Do not be afraid'.

Peter's response is typical. At first he is prepared to take a risk upon the word of Jesus. If it is Jesus, he will only have to call him across the water, and he will come (v. 28). At first he places his trust in the Lord, but then succumbs to the pressures of the storm around him. However, in this situation he calls on the help of the Lord, and Jesus holds him and keeps him safe (vv. 30-31). In Peter's situation of little faith and doubt, his Lord has stood by him. So it is with all the disciples in the boat. Jesus and Peter get into the boat, the wind drops and all confess: 'Truly, you are the Son of God' (v. 33).

In the experience of the disciples and Peter we find reflected the experience of every Christian. We often begin with the great courage which only faith can give us, but such courage of faith dwindles when wind and wave assail it. In this situation we remain ultimately dependent upon the gracious help of our Lord. Without Jesus we can make no headway. Jesus is the one who is close to God, who unfailingly looks to him for guidance and strength, while we go on with the everyday things in our lives, never giving our God a thought. Yet, when difficulties come God is there, coming out of the darkness into our lives. But even then our faith can falter. He sometimes asks us to do strange things: to jump out of the boat into the stormy water. Encouragingly, Peter's story — and the story of disciples who thought Jesus was only a ghost — tells us it is to those of little faith that Jesus still comes, holding us close and leading us into the safety and peace which only he can give.

TWENTIETH SUNDAY OF THE YEAR

Matthew 15:21-28

Scraps from the master's table

After Jesus' appearance to his disciples on the water (19th Sunday), he enters into conflict with 'Pharisees and Scribes from Jerusalem' over 'the tradition of the elders' (Mt 15:1). This encounter between a people who thinks they are God's good people because they have been chosen and have a Law and all its further interpretations and Jesus leads to anger. Jesus calls them 'hypocrites' (v. 7), and points out the falseness of their superficial claims to holiness (vv. 1-20). This is essential background to the Gospel of the Canaanite woman.

Jesus deliberately chooses to leave Gennesaret in Israel, to travel into the Gentile region of Tyre and Sidon (v. 21). He is walking away from the land regarded as God's land by its occupants. They were unable to see that holiness depended upon more than their own laws and smug religious self-satisfaction. In a Gentile land a Canaanite woman confesses her faith in Jesus as Son of David, and asks that he cure her daughter (v. 22). She is ignored: 'He answered her not a word' (v. 23). Only at the insistence of the disciples, because they are annoyed by her persistence (v. 23), does Jesus respond to the woman. He is unable to do anything for her as he was sent to 'the lost sheep of the House of Israel' (v. 24).

Jesus must first look to the children who have been called to the Master's table. But he rightly calls them 'the lost sheep of the House of Israel'. Matthew has told the story of their arrogant rejection of Jesus and his ways (vv. 10-20). They are indeed 'lost'. Jesus' ministry is directed to the perfection of the Law (see 5:17) not, as yet, to the Gentile mission. That will be a task which the risen Lord will give to his disciples (see 28:16-20).

But the response of the Gentile woman to Jesus is remarkable. She neither doubts nor questions what Jesus has said to her. Her needs drive her on: 'Lord, help me' (v. 25). This plea leads Jesus to harsher words, that it is not fair to take the children's food from the table and throw it to the house-dogs (v. 26). Her response to Jesus shows that she comes to him exactly as she is. She is aware of her nothingness; she is aware she can make no prior claims on God's goodness and mercy as dispensed by Jesus. However, in that awareness, she accepts her 'house-dog' role, waiting for the good things which might fall from the Master's table (v. 27). The children at the table, in their arrogant questioning of Jesus' ways (vv. 10-20), have discarded the food which Jesus offered them. In contrast to them, the woman is aware of the greatness of the Master, and the littleness of the one who receives. There can be no resistance to faith of this calibre: 'Let your wish be granted' (v. 28).

How often do we approach our God with selfish and self-centred demands that he do what we would like done? It is easy for us, privileged with a Christian formation and enjoying the fullness of a Christian sacramental life to think we deserve all the good things we have. In fact, at times we suspect that God does not recognise us enough! The example of Canaanite woman tells us that this is not the way to approach our God. We must be aware of our need to be filled; aware of what we are and who we are. Waiting expectantly and realistically, we can be filled with God's good gifts. In this way we too will merit praise: 'You have great faith' (v. 28).

TWENTY-FIRST SUNDAY OF THE YEAR

Matthew 16:13-20

The disciple who understands

At Caesarea Philippi Jesus asks: 'Who do people say the Son of Man is?' (Mt 16:13). In the Gospel according to Matthew Jesus' question to his disciples already contains a title: 'the Son of Man'. But the people pay no attention to the hint of that title. They are happy to settle for one of the precursors of the Messiah. The disciples respond to their Master's question that there is a variety of opinions about him. He might be John the Baptist, Elijah, Jeremiah or one of the Prophets (v. 14).

But what of the disciples themselves? Peter, in their name, makes a complete confession of faith: 'You are the Christ, the Son of the Living God' (v. 16). Adding to the title which was already in the question of Jesus, Peter points to Jesus as the Son of Man, the Christ and the Son of God. On this belief the Church is founded. The faith expressed in this confession is not mere words; it is a belief made visible in Peter, in the name of the people gathered around Jesus. Faith is not an idea. It is lived by people; it forms a Church.

Jesus' famous response to Peter's confession of faith tells us that Peter is the rock upon which the Church is built (v. 18). His faith is the basis of a journey through a long history and many cultures. Because of the faith of Peter, he is given a commission to lead the community through its long and complicated journey. The Prophet Isaiah had already spoken of 'the keys' as a symbol of authority. A wicked major-domo of the King's palace was replaced; the keys were given: 'I will place on his shoulder the key of the house of David (see Is 22:15-25). Thus Peter becomes the viceregent of a Church built upon a rock. He holds the keys, binding and loosing, interpreting God's ways in the world (v. 19).

One of the disciples has expressed a faith in Jesus of Nazareth which corresponds to the truth, but none of this is because of Peter himself: 'You are a happy man! Because it was not flesh and blood that revealed this to you but my Father in heaven' (v. 17). The disciple who is able to look through the apparent limitations of the man standing before him to make such a confession of faith does so in response to a gift from God. It was not his flesh and blood. It was the Father of Jesus who gifted him in this unique way. Not even the leader of the Apostles, the rock upon whom the Church was founded, the first of a long succession of pontiffs, can claim to be what he is because of his virtue and own inner strength and vision. As with all of us, such things are given to him by our good God.

The same Peter whose faith faltered when he was buffeted by the wind and the waves (see 14:22-33) has now shown that he is open to the gifts God gives him. For this he is blessed. We all know this is not the end of Peter's story. Whatever may happen through the ups and downs of a disciple's response, Peter shows that openness to the gift of the truth about Jesus leads to blessing. The faith of the Church and the faith of all who are happy to be part of it is the result of the gift of God. How much we depend upon God's good gifts! The important things in our lives come from God, and forgiveness when we fail to treasure such gifts also comes from God.

TWENTY-SECOND SUNDAY OF THE YEAR

Matthew 16:21-27

The disciple who fails to understand

How quickly the mighty fall! Only last week we rejoiced in the gift of understanding given to Peter (Mt 16:13-20). Today we read of his failure and his being cursed. Last week we read of his being the rock upon which the Church is founded (v. 18); today we read of his being the stone over which Jesus might stumble on his way to the Cross (v. 23). Peter is always 'rock', but he can be a rock upon which the Church can be founded, or a rock which leads it to stumble.

At Caesarea Philippi Jesus asked, 'Who do men say that the Son of Man is?' After Peter's confession, Jesus teaches his disciples that the Christ, the Son of the living God is still the Son of Man. The title 'the Son of Man' was a part of Jesus' question to Peter, and Jesus' being the Son of Man means that he must go on to Jerusalem to meet suffering and death. Throughout the Gospel, whenever Jesus speaks of the need to go to Jerusalem, to suffer, die and rise again, he always uses the expression 'the Son of Man' (see 16:21; 17:22-23; 20:17-19; 26:2).

Peter was able to understand that Jesus, the Son of Man, was the Christ, the Son of the living God, but he was unable to cope with Jesus' further teaching. It was impossible for Peter to accept that the Christ, the Son of the living God, would exercise his royal messiahship from the throne of a Cross. He thus attempts to stop Jesus' journey towards Jerusalem.

The story-teller goes to some trouble to show that Peter physically attempts to block Jesus' journey to Jerusalem.

It is not only a question of sharp words of disagreement. It is that, but it is more: 'Taking him aside, Peter started to remonstrate with him' (v. 22). His action and his words lead Jesus to address him as a stone over which he might stumble. Peter must take the place assigned to all true disciples: behind Jesus, following him towards Jerusalem: 'Get behind me' (v. 23).

Jesus is the Christ, the Son of the living God. However, he is not only that. He is also the Son of Man. He is among us as the one who serves, and who calls us to follow him down his way of loving service and gift of self. There is always the danger that Jesus might be understood as a glorious divine figure who somehow passed through the human story and thus saved us. This is a wrong, one-sided, understanding of Jesus which neglects his being our brother in both our joys and our sufferings.

There is also the further danger that, like Peter, the disciple might run the risk of telling Jesus the direction to take. Most of us would like God and his Son to be with us as we direct our own lives and establish our own agendas. Disciples must be followers of Jesus, never people who try to tell Jesus which way he must go. Thus, the disciple is also called to take up the Cross and follow Jesus (vv. 24-25). As Christ and Son of the living God, Jesus will be ultimately victorious through his loving gift of himself. However, such a victory belongs only to those who have been prepared to follow him down the way of the Son of Man. All of us, like Jesus, yearn for the glory which can be ours; but we are often not ready to pay the price of unconditional love.

TWENTY-THIRD SUNDAY OF THE YEAR

Matthew 18:15-20

See how they love one another

Today's Gospel is part of a discourse which Jesus gives to his followers on the way disciples should relate to one another. His words make demands that seem impossible in the hard-nosed world of today. Yet we are called to make these words of Jesus real.

When conflict arises over the injury we inevitably do to one another, then peace must be established by an encounter between the offended party and the offender (Mt 18:15). If this fails one should call upon the help of two or three other Christian witnesses so that the wrong can be set right and peace established within the community (v. 16). If this fails, the whole Christian community should be called upon to make a judgment (v. 17). The Christian offender who refuses to accept what the community decides is to be sent away from the community itself. He or she is arrogantly refusing to live by the basic law of Christianity: the law of love. But is this the end of the question. What is meant by 'treat him like a pagan or a tax collector' (v. 17)?

Matthew's Gospel was written to send the infant Church to the Gentiles to teach them (see 28:19), and in this Gospel Jesus shows a particular interest was shown in a tax collector named 'Matthew' (see 9:9; 10:3). Is the Christian who refuses the authority of the community to be shunned, or to be the subject of outreach and concern in imitation of a Jesus who was so interested in searching out tax collectors that he was called their friend (see 11:19)? As Jesus will shortly tell Peter, one must forgive one's brethren 'seventy-seven times', an infinite number of times (v. 22).

The Christian community has its own authority, but it is exercised in a way which proclaims that it flows from Jesus' new law of love. The members of the community should have a quality of life among them that makes people outside the community say: 'See how they love one another'. This must be preserved, as it repeats in Christian life, the life-style of Jesus himself: 'You must love one another as I have loved you' (John 13:34). Based on this love command, the binding and loosing in the community will reflect the binding and loosing which our God requires from us. Whatever its strengths and weaknesses, the Church's guidance and judgments in our own time are attempts to bind and loose in the pursuit of a love which imitates the love of Jesus.

To survive, the Church must be a society existing among other societies, but if we are to be true to Jesus, his life and his teaching, then we must sometimes act in a way that other institutions regard as foolishness. To search out and care for those who refuse the authority of the institution could be seen as suicidal, but that was the way of Jesus. The number of people who have turned away from the Church because they found it too forgiving is not large! Many have abandoned it because they found it unforgiving.

We will always need the presence of Jesus to give us the courage to love in such a way. That is why Jesus finishes his instructions with a command to constant prayer, and a reminder that when we gather together in his name, he is there in the midst of us (vv. 19-20).

TWENTY-FOURTH SUNDAY OF THE YEAR

Matthew 18:21-35

Compassion and forgiveness

Jesus' teaching about the need to settle conflict which we read last week was a surprising summons to the Christian Church to fly in the face of the accepted standards of judgment and condemnation. Peter is led to wonder just how generous he has to be. He thinks that he is being quite magnanimous in suggesting that he might forgive his brother or sister seven times (18:21). Seven is a perfect number, thus Peter is not being mean.

But Jesus' reply: 'Seventy-seven times' tells Peter that there is to be no end of forgiveness in the kingdom (v. 22). Peter felt that he could solve the problem by counting the number of times. Jesus and the Father whom he has come to make known do not work like that. But Peter is no longer simply Peter for the Gospel of Matthew. He is the rock of the Church (see 16:13-20). The instruction given to Peter is an instruction for the Church and especially an instruction for all those who lead in the Church.

The parable of the unforgiving debtor which follows stresses this point even further. Through the parable Jesus teaches that there must be a parallel between the abundance and unfailing forgiveness of God and the unfailing forgiveness of the members of God's household. A single talent was the largest unit of money known in the Near East, and ten thousand the largest number. Thus ten thousand talents is our 'billions of dollars' (v. 24)! Jesus is speaking in hyperbole, as it would be impossible for any servant to have such a debt, and even more impossible to ever pay it back.

Following the logic of a worldly-wise relationship between the person who lent the money and the person in debt, the Master moves to exact everything from him. Strangely, and quite wonderfully, he cancels the incredible debt as he 'felt so sorry for him' (v. 27). There is no reason for such an action except a deeply felt compassion which is acted upon.

The story of the relationship between the forgiven servant and his fellow servant is an exact parallel, except that now the debt is trivial and the servant's response to the request for time is outrageous. The inability and unwillingness of the servant to match his master's forgiveness are powerfully highlighted. Indeed, he moves in exactly the opposite direction. While the forgiveness of the Master was based upon compassion, the forgiven servant resorts to violence — 'he seized him by the throat and began to throttle him' (v. 28).

The whole household has seen what has happened, and stands in judgment upon their fellow servant. They draw the Master back into the story. He casts out the unforgiving servant, into the hands of the torturers. The Father abundantly forgives each member of his family, but this forgiveness remains conditional: 'do unto others as I have done unto you'. We cannot earn God's forgiveness, but we can lose it by jealously hoarding the blessings God gives us, and never sharing it with others by the quality of our own forgiveness. A person who does not forgive has never really experienced God's forgiveness. The household of God both experiences and dispenses the love of God in its forgiveness and compassion.

TWENTY-FIFTH SUNDAY OF THE YEAR

Matthew 20:1-16

Can I not do what I like?

Today's parable likens the kingdom of heaven to a landowner going out to hire workers for his vineyard (Mt 20:1). In the first instance, the landowner seeks out labourers for his vineyard, and offers them the usual daily wage of a denarius (v. 2). The contract for a given wage is struck only with the very first group of workers. Although the landowner will go to the market place and hire workers on four more occasions, no fixed wage is mentioned.

The landowner keeps returning to the market place to find further workers — at the third hour, the ninth hour, and even at the eleventh hour (vv. 3-7). Notice, however, that these later hired hands are offered no fixed sum. However, as he calls those standing idle in the market place at the third hour the issue of payment is again raised, but now in the more general terms of 'I will give you a fair wage' (v. 4). The issue of payment is still kept before the mind and imagination of the person reading or hearing the parable.

The moment is prepared in considerable detail. Clear instructions are given to the bailiff. The last to be employed are to be paid first, and the first are to come last (v. 8). The problem is that the promise made to those who were hired at the beginning of the day, the payment of a denarius, is the reward given to those who arrived at the eleventh hour.

One must imagine the queue, with the newly-arrived workers at the beginning, and those employed earlier, tired after a full day in the vineyard, watching them as they go off with their denarius. If we put ourselves in the place of those who are at the end of the queue, we can understand how they rightly expect to receive more than the agreed denarius. We can also share their disappointment and indignation when they do not (vv. 11-12).

This long story has only been told to prepare the reader for the final words of Jesus' parable. This is not another story about a man hiring workers. Jesus warned us of that from his very first words: 'The kingdom of heaven is like . . .' (v. 1). The point is: it is God's kingdom. He will decide how this kingdom will be administered, and of one thing we can be certain: it will not be administered in the same way as any earthly kingdom. Measured by the principles of established custom, the people who worked longer should have been paid more. That is the way we would do it . . . but does God work that way?

Should we not allow God to be God? Jesus' teaching about the kingdom subverts our established order. It surprises us, because the God of Jesus is a God of surprises. The master of the vineyard has not been unjust . . . he has been extraordinarily generous. It is this strange and unexpected generosity which creates the problem. Those who think they can calculate exactly how God must act are in for a surprise. Yet, God's plan is to bring delight and fulfilment to everyone. All who work in the Lord's vineyard should be delighted that some receive what is just, while others have been blessed with God's great generosity. Who are we to question why? Can God not do what he likes with his love? Even the grumbler is called 'My friend' (v. 13).

TWENTY-SIXTH SUNDAY OF THE YEAR

Matthew 21:28-32

Saying and doing

The setting of today's parable is Jesus speaking to 'the chief priests and the elders of the people'. A great deal has happened in the story since last Sunday's Gospel, but it has not been reported in the Lectionary. Jesus is now in Jerusalem. He has entered the city (Mt 21:1-11) and taken possession of the Temple, driving out all who would make his House a robber's den (21:12-17). The crisis point of Jesus' ministry has arrived. He will enter into conflict with the established religious authorities, forcing them to exercise judgment upon themselves.

He tells 'the chief priests and the elders of the people' (see 21:23) a parable of two sons, one of whom says he will not work in the vineyard, but eventually does and the other who is full of promises, but does not act to make the promises a reality (vv. 28-30). As always with Jesus' parables, the sting is in the tail of the story, as he asks his critical listeners: 'Which of the two did the father's will' (v. 31), but he had already warned them that this question would be posed. The story opened with Jesus' earlier question: 'What is your opinion?' (v. 28).

They rightly choose the former son as the one who 'did the will of his Father'. Jesus has led his audience, so critical of what he has said and done, especially in his driving out of the vendors from the Temple (see vv. 12-17), to make their own decision on the way to do the Father's will. It is not a question of mouthing the right words and going through the right rituals; one is called to actually do what the Father wants.

Jesus continues his discussion with the religious and political leaders of Israel by pointing to those people who had come before him, but whom these established authorities rejected, starting from John the Baptist vv. 31-32). He was not believed, even though he came preaching the way of righteousness. Not only did he preach righteousness, however; he lived it. Jesus describes him as 'a pattern of true righteousness' (v. 32). This man who both preached and lived righteousness was killed, but the broken people, the tax collectors and the prostitutes accepted what he had to bring. They believed him, repented, and thus entered the kingdom of heaven. But not even the wholeness given to the broken has touched the hearts of the establishment. They saw it happening, but did not themselves repent (v. 32).

Jesus is attacking the so-called 'religious people' who go through the motions of being God-directed people, mouthing the right words and performing the right rituals, but not putting their lives where their words are. In the Western world, Christian standards had gradually become the accepted values. In our rapidly changing and increasingly secularised world they no longer play this role in society at large. It is only through lives which speak to a society in danger of losing its soul that Christianity will give evidence of the kingdom. If we Church-goers, who listen to the Gospel, are not doing what we are saying, where can the so-called sinners of our time place their hope and trust? This is a challenge to go to the maverick fringe of society, joining the tax collectors and prostitutes as they make their way into the kingdom (v. 31).

TWENTY-SEVENTH SUNDAY OF THE YEAR

Matthew 21:33-43

Losing the kingdom

Looking back to an image used by the prophet Isaiah to speak of the people of God and their land (see Is 5:1-2), Jesus continues to speak to 'the chief priests and the elders of the people'. Jesus tells of a landowner who plants the vineyard and fences it (Mt 21:33). The contact with Isaiah 5 makes it clear that the vineyard is the true Israel, established through the careful intervention of God.

But once the vineyard was ready to produce its fruit, it is left to others to administer and to have it produce the good fruit. God as Lord and the religious authorities as his temporary administrators are close to the surface of the parable. The listeners themselves would be well aware from their Jewish traditions that they were caring for the vineyard of the Lord.

At harvest time the master asks that the fruits of the vintage come to him (v. 34). He is the master and lord, and justly asks for this. Thus far the story follows a familiar pattern, but Jesus looks back to the experience of the prophets in Israel. Those entrusted with the vineyard of the Lord have not been loyal to their lord and master. The servants of the Lord had continually gone to the people asking them to produce good fruits, but they suffered beatings, death and stoning (vv. 35-36).

In a final attempt to bring those entrusted with the care and administration of his vineyard into a right relationship with himself, the master sends his son (v. 37). The reference to Jesus himself, well-known for his practice of calling God his Father, would not have been missed. If the story of Israel's treatment of the prophets as the servants of the Lord lay behind the way in which the servants of the parable have been treated, then Jesus' listeners would now be aware that he was claiming to be the son, sent by God, the Lord of Israel. The parable reports that the tenants, anxious to take possession of the inheritance of the son, seize him, throw him out of the vineyard and kill him (vv. 38-39).

The veil of symbols is torn away with Jesus' question: 'When the owner of the vineyard comes, what will he do to those tenants?' (v. 40). They will come to a violent end, and the vineyard will be given to others (v. 43). All this, however, is yet to happen. The parable has shifted from a story telling of events from the past into a prediction of what will happen in the future. First the Son must be taken out of the city and slain. The Cross is close at hand, but that rejected stone will become the keystone to a new building — the new people of God to whom the vineyard will be entrusted.

This is not a story from the past. We are reading this Gospel in the Church today. Jesus warns us that prophets call us to fruitfulness, but we too run the danger of killing them. In our self-sufficiency we too can sit comfortably in a vineyard we think is ours. One day we may find that it has been taken from us, and given to those whom we may not have considered worthy. We will only have ourselves to blame.

TWENTY-EIGHTH SUNDAY OF THE YEAR

Matthew 22:1-14

Invitation to a wedding

The series of parables which Jesus directs against the leaders of Israel continues. Jesus speaks to 'the chief priests and elders of the people'. This week's parable likens the kingdom of heaven 'to a king who gave a feast for his son's wedding' (Mt 22:1-2). Often in the Bible the rich symbolism of a wedding feast, with its abundance of wine, food and a union of love, is used to speak of God's taking final possession of his people. Here the symbol is directed not just to any wedding but to a wedding given by a king for his son.

The theme of Jesus' being the son, sent by the Lord of the vineyard was the theme of last week's parable (see 21:33-46). The biblical image of the wedding feast, the traditional understanding of God as 'king' and Jesus' claims to be the one sent by God as his son tell the reader that the presence of Jesus to his people is the moment of God's taking possession of his people.

There are so many excuses for not attending the wedding. As with the parable of the wicked vinekeepers, the king sends his servants, but they are rejected, as those invited have other interests: a farm or a business (vv. 4-5). Indeed, these other attractions are so powerful that the wedding seems to be a bit of a threat. The best way to escape this threat is to kill the messengers who bring the invitation. Once again, Israel's troubled relationship with God forms the background to the story of the servants of the king. Long have they maltreated and killed the servants, the prophets of the Lord.

But the king will always be the king. He will have the last word. Thus, his anger is roused, and the chosen guests are slain and their town is destroyed (v. 7). In their place come 'everyone you can find'. The wedding feast is no longer the gathering of a chosen people. It is the place where God takes possession of all peoples (vv. 8-10). The early Church, reading this story, looks back upon the destruction of Jerusalem and the beginnings of the mission of Christianity into the Gentile world as the fulfilment of this parabolic prophecy of Jesus.

But being chosen does not necessarily lead to the acceptance of the one who chose you. It is not good enough simply to be there. Someone comes in dirty clothing, symbolising a life that has undergone no change — not even for the wedding (v. 11). The king approaches him and calls him 'friend', but receives no answer (v. 12). This participant at the wedding has no desire to respond to the wishes of the king. He must be cast out. He has been called, but failed in his response to that call (vv. 13-14).

Today's parable echoes the controversies between Jesus and his Jewish opponents, but it leads us beyond that debate. It shows us God's gracious calling of all of us from the highways and the by-ways into the richness which his life and love can offer. But it also warns us that Christian life is a web made up of interaction between God's gracious invitation and our free response. If our response does not take God's invitation seriously, it is already the wrong response.

TWENTY-NINTH SUNDAY OF THE YEAR

Matthew 22:15-21

Render to God

Jesus' entry into Jerusalem and his taking possession of the Temple has led to a series of parables through which he attacks the political and religious leaders of Israel. He has always held the initiative. Now that changes. Having been on the receiving end of Jesus' thinly veiled attacks through the parables, the Pharisees attempt to put Jesus into a no-win situation. The telling of the story, however, already places the Pharisees in a bad light. They go away from the conflict 'to work out between them how to trap him' (v. 15). They do not have the courage to face Jesus themselves. They 'send their disciples to him, together with the Herodians' (v. 16). This itself is an unholy alliance between the defenders of the tradition (the Pharisees and their disciples) and the royal party who worked in league with the Romans (the Herodians).

The messengers praise his teaching 'the way of God in an honest way' (v. 16). Jesus does indeed speak the truth. In fact, this is what will lead him to the Cross. The trap they are setting is an attempt to lead him to that Cross. They ask whether one should pay taxes to Caesar (v. 17). This question could place Jesus in a no-win situation. If Jesus answers 'yes', then he will be guilty of disloyalty to the Jewish people, represented by the messengers of the Pharisees; if he says 'no', then he will be guilty of fomenting rebellion against Rome, represented by the Herodians.

Jesus sees through their malice and hypocrisy, and tells them so. He asks for the denarius, the coin used to pay the tax (v. 19). He does not carry it, but his opponents are quite willing to use Caesar's money in their business transactions. It is a tacit acceptance of Caesar's system. As they are willing to carry the coin which carries Caesar's effigy (v. 20), they should also be willing to give back to Caesar what is his. But there is a further duty beyond rendering to Caesar what is his. They are obliged to recognise the supreme Sovereign (v. 21).

As our Gospel readings over the past weeks have shown, since Jesus arrived in Jerusalem there have been continual conflicts between himself and the Jewish authorities. Thus, it is their second obligation — rendering to God — which needs their attention. They should be worrying less about what is due to Caesar, and paying more attention to the presence of the Son of God in their midst.

Politics and religion mix rather uncomfortably, yet politics and religion there will always be. It is not a question of naively forgetting one or the other. It is a question of putting first things first. Politics which look to the service of the supreme Sovereign will work, but a service of God which is dominated by politics can only bring hatred and sinfulness into the Church. These principles, so clearly enunciated in today's encounter between Jesus and representatives of both religious authority (Pharisees) and political authority (Herodians), not only challenge the state to allow God to be God, but especially challenge the Church to preach and live the Gospel of Jesus Christ, rather than the Gospel of political convenience.

THIRTIETH SUNDAY OF THE YEAR

Matthew 22:34-40

The greatest commandments

The angry encounters between Jesus and his opponents come to a conclusion in today's Gospel. In a final attack, the Pharisees attempt to show Jesus' lack of professional knowledge of the Law. He has shown how they are repeating the traditional unfaithfulness of the custodians of the Lord's vineyard, and he has caught them out in their double standards, so now they turn to the Law. In theory, all the commandments were to be observed with equal seriousness. However, within the 613 commandments of the Law there had developed an understanding of the lighter and the heavier commandments. The scholars and scribes argued over these distinctions. The Pharisees now attempt to trap Jesus into making a damaging statement within this learned discussion (Mt 22:34).

Jesus cuts the ground from under their feet. They could not possibly argue with Jesus' answer. The first part of his response comes from the Book of Deuteronomy (Deut 6:5), and is central to Jewish faith: 'You must love the Lord your God with all your heart, with all your soul and with all your mind' (v. 37). The love of God is the first of all the commandments. But there is also a second commandment which is like the first: 'You must love your neighbour as yourself' (v. 39). This is also a part of the Jewish tradition, coming to them from the Book of Leviticus (Lev 19:18, 34).

Laws 'hang upon' Old Testament passages in the Jewish tradition. Rabbinic discussions look back to the biblical books as the source and explanation of laws which have developed to meet the developing needs of God's people. Jesus now claims that the whole of the will of God in Scripture hangs upon, is derived from and is summed up in, the double command of love. What God wills is love. All individual commands and obligations must be measured against and judged by the canon of love.

But if it is all summed up in laws that were already found in the Old Testament, what has Jesus introduced into the human story which was not already present? The newness of Jesus' approach has not been to invent the two basic laws. They came to him from his Jewish background. His originality has been to place the love of God and the love of neighbour together. It is impossible to love God and hate your neighbour, and equally impossible to give yourself in love to your neighbour, and claim that you have no love of God. God and the human situation are intimately interwoven, however conscious we are of that truth. This is nowhere more clearly shown than in Jesus of Nazareth, Son of Man and Son of God, but it should also be shown in the love of all who claim to be followers of Jesus.

Today's Gospel represents the last argument between Jesus and the teachers of Israel. As we come to the end of a long series of Gospel readings dealing with the clash between Jesus and the false religious practice of the Pharisees, we should remember that the Gospel is read in our liturgy to challenge us, to help us understand better Jesus' way to God. As Jesus argues and teaches through these passages, he is arguing with us and teaching us. There is a Pharisee in each one of us, and we all need to come down from our religious pedestals to learn that there are only two commandments which, in reality, are one: to love God and love our neighbour.

THIRTY-FIRST SUNDAY OF THE YEAR

Matthew 23:1-12

You have only one father

Matthew has Jesus turn to both the people and his disciples to draw his lesson from conflict between himself and the religious leaders of Israel. Matthew's own Christian community were reading this Gospel story — not the Pharisees (Mt 23:1). Today's Gospel reading is not primarily an attack on the Pharisees, as it may appear. It is above all an address to the people and Jesus' disciples. It is instruction, not vitriol.

Jesus speaks out against the hypocrisy of authorities who have received the authentic tradition of the word of God, but who do not live according to that tradition (vv. 2-3). The word that such people proclaim remains valid, just as their office as the teachers of the Word, occupying the chair of Moses, is valid. Because of the intrinsic validity of the Word itself and the office of teacher, the Scribes and the Pharisees must be listened to. But the lives they live must never guide the people and the disciples: 'they do not practise what they preach' (v. 3).

The Christian is always summoned to follow Jesus. This means both preaching and living the authentic word of God. True religion never parades its virtues, it spends itself in giving life to others through loss of self in generous loving.

The Synagogue had its Rabbis, Fathers and Teachers. Many of the members of Matthew's community had come into Christianity from the Synagogue. They had come to believe that Jesus was the Christ, the Son of God, and they had crossed the road from the secure traditions of Israel into the newness of faith in Jesus Christ. Understandably some people from Matthew's community envied the Rabbis, the Fathers and the Teachers of the Synagogue. They were figures with authority. Some would have liked to repeat this safe structure within the Christian community.

Jesus tells them it must not be so within Christianity (vv. 8-9). There must be no bowing and scraping to human figures who take on the roles which the Christians once knew when they were in the Synagogue. They had 'crossed the road' from established ways into a Christian community. The old structures could no longer hold, because they now lived in a new world. In that world, which is also ours as we continue to live in the Christian community, there can be only one Master, one Father, one Teacher: the Christ (v. 9).

The words of Jesus are disturbingly subversive when proclaimed courageously and heard with courage in the contemporary Christian Church. We do have our 'Fathers'. We even have our 'Eminences', 'Lords' and 'Your Graces', and there are some to whom these titles of honour and public recognition of authority are important. Titles, in themselves, mean little. It is the person behind the title, which always has some historical explanation, who is important. The lesson we learn from both the words and life of Jesus is clear: the gift of self in humble and loving service is the only way to reflect what God has done for us. If we practise what we preach (v. 3) the presence or absence of titles will become irrelevant (vv. 8-10).

THIRTY-SECOND SUNDAY OF THE YEAR

Matthew 25:1-13

The now and the not yet

As the Gospel of Matthew draws towards the end of Jesus' public ministry, the themes of delay and the need to be ready for the final coming of the Lord become important. Although, as we have seen over the Paschal Season, Matthew presents the death and resurrection as the 'turning point of the ages', when heaven and earth pass away (see Mt 5:17-18; 27:51-53; 28:2-4), his community is still well aware that heaven and earth are in their usual place. The paschal events are behind them, but the community understands that their own history lies ahead of them. The Christian Church may have to live its life in imitation of Christ through a long history, but it must always remember that in the end, he will return as the Lord of all history.

The setting for the parable of the ten bridesmaids is strongly reminiscent of oriental wedding practices. The ten virginal bridesmaids are an escort of honour appointed to greet the bridegroom when he returns from the house of the bride, bringing his bride with him (25:1). The problems of the wedding contract and the unhurried exchange of gifts inevitably led to long delays. The virgins, some better equipped than others, wait with their lamps alight for this evening celebration, to play their role in the joyful procession (vv. 2-4).

The contrast between the five wise and the five foolish virgins is that the wise ones reckon with the possibility of a delay. The unwise virgins fail to anticipate such a delay, and thus find themselves unprepared when the groom eventually arrives (vv. 7-8). To share the oil would have meant that all the lamps would go out, and the welcoming ceremony would be a failure. Thus 'those who were ready' escort the groom (v. 10), while the others seek oil (v. 9). On their return, calling out 'Lord, Lord', they are told that they are not known.

The parable leads inevitably to the final words of Jesus: 'Stay awake, because you do not know either the day or the hour' (v. 13). This story, which probably comes from popular folk tales, has been retold in the Gospel of Matthew to warn against making too much of the 'now' and forgetting that the 'not yet' is an essential part of the Christian life.

In its present form Jesus' parable speaks strongly to our need to live our present with an eye on the future. The tendency to live our own history as if it were the only one that mattered is within us all. Most of us have a tendency to live as if either the 'now' is the only important thing, while some ignore the joys, sufferings and responsibilities of the 'now' and simply wait for God's final solution in the 'not yet'. Both approaches to the Christian life leave us unprepared for the God of surprises who has his own plans for our todays and our tomorrows. Christian living can never settle for the present, nor can it simply wait idly for the future coming of God. It must be deeply committed to God's gift of the present, waiting for God's future gifts, and his final coming; and prepared to take all the risks of following his Son, Jesus of Nazareth, through the time in between.

THIRTY-THIRD SUNDAY OF THE YEAR

Matthew 25:14-30

Living the in-between time

The parable of the wise and foolish virgins warned against not being ready for the delay. It was an introduction to the theme of living the in-between time. In today's Gospel Jesus moves on from the parable of the wise and foolish virgins to develop further what it means to be watchful and faithful during the time of waiting.

Each of the characters in the parable plays an important role, but the central figure is 'the man on his way abroad' (Mt 25:14). There is a Master who will be away for some time, but who will eventually return. In the meantime, he entrusts three servants with certain responsibilities. The three servants are entrusted with talents given to them by their Master (v. 15). The word 'talent', in the parable, means money, not one's skills. It was a standard measure of weight in the Near East. A talent is a large sum of money. In fact, the servants have been given a treasure. The men with the five and the two talents trade with them (vv. 16-17). Using the interest which they raise, the treasure is doubled. The third servant, paralysed by the fear of taking a risk, hides the money (v. 18).

On the Master's return the servants who traded and doubled their treasure are praised and rewarded (vv. 19-23). The anxiety-ridden servant is condemned because he is wicked and lazy. Referring to the demanding nature of the Master, he tries to excuse why he behaved as he did: out of fear of failure he has refused even to try. He knew that the Master was an exacting Lord and demanded performance from his servants. He condemns himself by not responding to the demands of the Master (vv. 24-27).

Jesus' parable stresses the seriousness of his demands. The fear-ridden servant who would not move, is stripped of everything. But the parable has a strange ending which sometimes seems to contradict other passages in the Gospel where Jesus shows so much concern for the poor and deprived. In this parable, the rich get richer and the fear-ridden poor man is reduced to nothing (vv. 27-28). Why should the rich get richer?

A disciple who responds fully to the gift God has given him will receive still greater gifts. Growth in the kingdom of God which Jesus has established among us can only be gained by risk and effort. Miserliness and fear will never bring the rich benefits of the kingdom. Exercise brings strength, fear and laziness bring only death. As always, the teaching of Jesus subverts an established order which spends great time and energy looking after itself and defending its self-righteousness. Such behaviour is parallel to digging a hole in the ground and hiding the Master's talent (see v. 18).

Once we are aware that there is an all-important 'in-between' time in the Christian life, we must take it seriously. It cannot be lived locked away within our own securities. We have been given a treasure to be used. To be a Christian means to be a missionary. To sit locked up in fear, awaiting the return of a stern Master, is to commit oneself to self-destruction. He is rich in his bountiful gift of 'talents' . . . but asks that we exercise them with joy and courage.

CHRIST THE KING

Matthew 25:31-46

The sheep and the goats

There are many ways in which Jesus is our universal King. One of the most important of them is his role as judge. Some details in Matthew's story of the final judgment could distract us from its central point: the majesty of the Son of Man coming with all the angels as judge, the fact of a final reckoning, the separation of the sheep and the goats. These important features of the story serve to present the real question: what is the criterion of judgment?

However important the in-between time may be, it cannot take away from the central truth that the Son of Man, the one who suffered but was raised, will come again in glory as judge (Mt 25:31-32). Only Matthew describes the final judgment in such concrete and practical terms. Using the imagery of sheep and goats, he presents the final division of the blessed from cursed as the result of our behaviour during the 'in-between time'.

The blessed ones, sheep gathered from all the nations and at the right hand of the King, inherit the kingdom (v. 34). They are rewarded for their care of Jesus present in the hungry, the thirsty, the stranger, the naked, the sick and the imprisoned (vv. 35-40). Though ignorant of Jesus' presence in the broken people of society, they cared for them nevertheless. Exactly the same criterion is used to curse the goats, equally gathered from the nations but at the left hand of the King. They are cursed, and sent into eternal fire, an image taken from Jewish traditional language as the place of final punishment. They have not accepted the presence of Jesus in the hungry, the thirsty, the stranger, the naked, the sick and the imprisoned. They too were ignorant of the harm they did to Jesus himself, but their behaviour towards the least of those who were members of his family has led to their self-condemnation.

Earlier in the Gospel of Matthew, Jesus taught that the whole of the Law could be summed up in love of God and love of neighbour (see 22:34-40). The final judgment is based upon that new Law, but it is now applied uncompromisingly to situations of everyday life. The final question will be: did you love me through your love of the poor in concrete acts of mercy? The risen Jesus is not only alive in the faith of the Church and in the good things that happen to us. He is also present to us in those around us who ask for our help. 'In so far as you did this to one of the least of these brethren of mine, you did it to me' (vv. 40, 45).

Jesus is our universal King. The Gospel of Matthew shows that he exercises his kingship by choosing us, but by then setting us free so that we might return to him as his responsible daughters and sons at the end of time. Christ is a King who has given us the offer of life but we are responsible for it. He takes each one of us seriously, and he asks that we take his offer of life and freedom equally seriously by sharing his love with those around us who are less fortunate. How will the present generation be judged? How will I be judged? How do I treat the least of those who are members of the family of Jesus who look to me for affection, care and support? Will I be judged as a sheep or a goat? Although the characters in the Gospel story did not know that Jesus was present in the least of the members of his family, I do know. I have read the story!

FEASTS WHICH MAY OCCUR ON A SUNDAY

THE PRESENTATION OF THE LORD

Luke 2:22-40

Salvation for the nations

Mary, Joseph, Simeon and Anna all stand righteous before the Lord: 'upright and devout' (Lk 2:25). Each one comes at the end of a long story of faithfulness, waiting for the fulfilment of the promises made to Israel. In Old Testament terms, the great characters from Jesus' infancy story are the best fruits of Israel's history. They are the 'poor of Jahweh', not rich in this world's possessions, but placing all their hope and trust in the saving intervention of God. Everything they do indicates this: the parents of Jesus go to Jerusalem to present him to the Lord (v. 22), Simeon is looking for Israel's comforting and full of the Holy Spirit (v. 25) and Anna never leaves the Temple (v. 37), looking forward to the deliverance of Jerusalem (v. 38).

But the time of waiting has come to an end. Yet, the presentation of Jesus, Mary's first-born, does not break with the Law. The Word of God, as it has been communicated to Israel through the Law, must be fulfilled. Mary has now said 'yes' to the request that the Word of God take place in and through her (see Lk 1:38). Simeon takes the fruit of her womb, the child Jesus, in his arms and in the name of the whole of Israel's waiting proclaims: 'Now, Lord, you can let your servant go in peace . . . because my eyes have seen the salvation which you have prepared for all the nations to see' (2:29-31). These are not simply the words of a God-fearing man reflecting his own impressions. Simeon, in the name of the old order, welcomes salvation for all the nations.

The parents of Jesus are unable to understand all that is being said (v. 33), and Mary is told that while her son will create division in Israel, where some will accept him and others fail to do so, she herself will be called to decide, and a sword will pierce her heart (vv 34-35). Anna, who has never left the Temple day and night, now proclaims to all Jerusalem that this child brings the deliverance of Jerusalem (v. 38).

A tiny family sets out from the Temple, awe-struck with the incredible things that have been happening around them. Little wonder that Simeon promises Mary that a sword would pierce her heart. She has said her 'yes' to God, but she must keep on saying it. The journey of Jesus and his family is just beginning. It will only continue if they are all — Jesus included — prepared to take the risk of saying 'yes' to God.

Today's Feast highlights the perfection of the Law of God. But now another period of God's presence to his people has begun. Jesus is the fruit of Mary's 'yes' to God, and we are the fruit of a further 'yes'. Jesus has asked each and every one of us to follow him, and the Christian lives which we live are our positive response to him. Perhaps we often hesitate. Our response is neither 'yes' nor 'no', but rather 'y-o?'. On this day made possible by the never-failing positive response from Jesus, Mary and Joseph, symbolised by the fulfilment of the demands of the Law that he be presented in the Temple, may we be encouraged by the bewildered family that walked away from the Temple. May we find direction and purpose — as they did — in an unshakeable trust in our good God and Father.

THE BIRTH OF JOHN THE BAPTIST

Luke 1:5-17, 66-80

His name is John

Elizabeth and Zechariah play a key role at the beginning of the Gospel of Luke. They have been described as 'righteous before God, walking in all the commandments and ordinances of the law blameless' (Luke 1:6). They are perfect models of the holiness which comes from the observance of the Covenant. Yet they are without child.

God fills their emptiness, even in their old age. Now they are no longer a part of the former story of a people preparing for the coming of the Messiah. They belong to the new story: the story of Jesus. The signs and wonders which have accompanied the annunciation to Zechariah show that something new is happening in the story of God's people.

Signs and wonder now fill the days of his birth and his naming. The birth of the child itself shows that with God nothing is impossible. Even though he never appears in the story, God is one of its chief characters. He has a plan, and there will be different reactions to it. The name to be chosen is impossible. The friends and neighbours point this out: 'No one in your family has that name' (1:61). They represent the way things used to be done. But something new is happening here, and the old ways cannot contain it.

Despite their belonging to the old order, both Elizabeth and Zechariah have been caught up into the plan of God, and respond generously to it. Elizabeth has no hesitation in telling the neighbours and relations: 'He is to be called John' (v. 60). Zechariah: 'His name is John' (v. 62), and immediately his tongue is freed. The name has already been given through the word of God, communicated by the angel of the Lord, in the annunciation to Zechariah: 'Your wife Elizabeth is to bear you a son and you must name him John' (1:13).

Although omitted in our Gospel reading, the first thing Zechariah does with his restored power of speech is sing praise to God in his famous hymn, the *Benedictus:* 'Blessed be the Lord, the God of Israel, for he has visited his people' (v. 68). God has entered the human story. He had made his ways known through the marvels surrounding the birth and the naming of John the Baptist.

How should one react to these marvels? Some were simply filled with awe. Some talked about it. Some treasured it in their hearts (vv. 65-66). They waited, treasuring these mysteries of the strange new action of God in their lives, until such time as their full meaning would become clear. This mixed reaction to the presence of God in certain events in the human story does not alter the facts announced by the story-teller: 'The hand of the Lord was with him'. Whatever human response may be, the hand of the Lord directs the story of our salvation. John the Baptist is an important part of that story.

The surprising newness of our God should be always with us, exhilarating and challenging us each day. There are two different stories in our lives which intersect. One is the story of God's marvellous action, and the other is the story of our day-to-day lives. Are we able to read the wonders of God as he enters our day to day ordinariness? How do we react to his presence? Are we awestruck into inactivity, do we merely talk about it, or do we treasure these mysteries in our hearts?

PETER AND PAUL

Matthew 16:13-19

Flesh and blood has not revealed this

Down through the centuries of the Christian Church, Matthew's story of Peter's confession has been told and retold. As he begins his final journey towards Jerusalem, Jesus asks the disciples: 'Who do people say the Son of Man is?' (Mt 16:13). In the Gospel of Matthew the words of Jesus already contain a title: 'the Son of Man'. It is not entirely clear who 'the Son of Man' might be, but the people pay no attention to the hints of a title. They simply ignore the enigmatic title, happy to settle for one of the precursors of the Messiah: John the Baptist, Elijah, Jeremiah or one of the Prophets (v. 14). Jesus is not the Messiah, but he is an important figure, fulfilling the promises to Israel, that before the days of the Messiah a figure would come to prepare his way.

Jesus makes no judgment upon this understanding of the people. He turns to the disciples, and asks: 'Who do you say that I am?' (v. 16). Notice that the term 'the Son of Man' has now been replaced by 'I'. Jesus is the Son of Man. Peter, in their name, adds to this title as he makes his confession of faith: 'You are the Christ, the Son of the Living God' (v. 16).

In these few verses Jesus is presented as the Son of Man, the Christ and the Son of God. It is on this belief that the Church is founded, but a belief made visible in Peter, in the name of the people gathered around Jesus. Faith is not an idea. Jesus challenges the people who follow him to both confess and live their belief. As St. Paul tells the Romans: 'If you confess with your lips that

Jesus is Lord and believe in your heart that God raised him from the dead, you will be saved' (Rom 10:9). The Christian faith is proclaimed and lived by a Christian people; it forms a Church.

Jesus' famous response to Peter's confession of faith tells us that Peter is the rock upon which the Church is built (Mt 16:18). His faith is the basis of a journey through a long history and many cultures. Peter is also the teacher, the one who holds the keys, binding and loosing, interpreting authoritatively God's ways in the world (v. 19). For those of us from the Catholic tradition, these words give us a sure guide and trust in the unfailing presence of Jesus in the pilgrim Church.

But what must not be forgotten is that none of this is because of Peter himself: It was not flesh and blood which revealed this to you, but my Father in heaven' (v. 17). The fact that there was a Peter, and that today we still have a Peter, in the person of the Holy Father, is a gift of God. It was not and is not the flesh and blood of a human being; it is not because of some inherent human authority invested in a man. It was and is the Father of Jesus who gifted the community of believers in this unique way.

Our faith is a gift of God, our Church is a gift of God, our leadership is a gift of God. Everything in our dealings with God, his Son Jesus and the life of the Spirit, is pure gift. Let us keep this truth clearly in mind lest we come to think that the Church and its administration of the mysteries of the Gods's gifts to us can be manipulated into yet another power structure, following the ways of flesh and blood.

THE TRANSFIGURATION

Matthew 17:1-9

No place to pitch a tent

Throughout the latter part of the Gospel of Matthew, Jesus begins to warn his disciples that he is going up to Jerusalem, and there he must suffer many things, be killed, and rise again (see Mt 16:13-28; 17:22-23; 20:17-19). But as Jesus moves towards his death, the journey to Jerusalem and death is strangely interrupted by an unexpected moment of glory.

He takes three disciples to the top of a mountain (Mt 17:1). Since the experience of Sinai, mountains are places where God makes himself known. Before their eyes he is transfigured. The description of the transfigured form of Jesus comes from the language which Jewish thinkers were using to speak of the appearance of the Messiah at the end of time (v. 2). The final appearance of the Messiah in glory is partially experienced on the mountain. In the middle of a journey towards suffering, Jesus appears before three of his disciples as the glorious Messiah.

But the disciples witness not only the transfigured Jesus. 'Suddenly' Moses and Elijah are there, in conversation with him (v. 3). The Law, the Prophets and Jesus are one. The disciples find themselves at the crossroads of God's salvation history. The Law established a covenant with a chosen people. The prophets performed the task of continually reminding the people of the covenant and of chastising them in their unfaithfulness. Both the Law and the prophets looked forward to God's final intervention into the human story. The disciples are witnesses to that intervention.

The disciples have a problem, however. They would like to stop God's history. Peter suggests that tents be set up so that this moment of truth can be held, a static vision for all to behold (v. 4). He is happy to settle for that particular truth-filled moment. This cannot be. While he is still making this suggestion a voice from the clouds affirms that Jesus is the Son of God. Indeed, he is the beloved Son of God. This means that the way in which he responds to God makes him special. He enjoys God's favour, but if the disciples are to fully understand all that is happening in and through Jesus they must listen to his voice (v. 5).

The excitement of being with Moses, Elijah and the glorious Messsiah turns into fear. The glory disappears. A person who is now 'only Jesus' touches them, encourages them, and together they descend the mountain. On the way down the mountain he hints that the glory which they have briefly experienced will only be his through the experience of suffering and death: 'risen from the dead'.

The Church proclaims the story of the transfiguration to teach us that there is no place for the disciple of Jesus to pitch a tent, to dwell on the moments of success and truth which occasionally come our way. We too are privileged to stand within God's salvation history: between the givenness of the Law, the prophets and the life, death and resurrection of Jesus. At times we are touched by hints of the glory which lies ahead, but to settle for 'the seeds of the promise' while still on the journey would be to miss the promise itself. We must follow a suffering Jesus along a way of the Cross to come to the glory.

Luke 1:39-56

The almighty has done great things

Stories of the action of God in the lives of Zechariah and his wife Elizabeth, who will have a son in her old age (see Lk 1:5-25) and in the life of Mary of Nazareth, who will have a son as a virgin-mother (see 1:26-38) precede today's Gospel. It is important to be aware of the experience which the two women have already had in Luke's story as we come to read of their encounter in the Visitation.

Two mothers meet. The Mother of John, the Precursor, meets the Mother of Jesus, the Christ, the Son of God. The younger woman greets her cousin, and the greeting fills Elizabeth with the Holy Spirit. The child Elizabeth has been nurturing in her womb for six months quickens, and Elizabeth cries out her joy. She salutes Mary as the most blessed of all women, and blessed also is the fruit of her womb. How could she have known that her unmarried younger cousin was pregnant? Such questions are idle, as this is a question about the action of God in human affairs.

Her own experience of the Spirit and the quickening of the child in her womb leads Elizabeth to recognise the dignity of Mary, and the dignity of the child she is bearing. Even though Jesus has not been born, he is given the title of 'Lord': 'Why should I be honoured with a visit from the mother of my Lord' (1:43). Yet it is the wonder of Mary, the first of all believers, that is acclaimed. Elizabeth sings Mary's praise in the light of her response to God's intervention in her life, known to the reader of the Gospel from the immediately previous account of the Annunciation: 'Blessed is she who believed that the promise made her by the Lord would be fulfilled' (v. 45).

There is nothing in the encounter between Elizabeth and Mary that is out of place. The delicacy and respect which both women show towards one another, and the praise which Elizabeth gives to Mary are perfect and coherent with the story of the Gospel so far. Yet, in her famous Magnificat, Mary points away from herself towards the God who stands behind all that has been reported. The message of Mary's canticle is found in her confession that she is his 'lowly handmaid' (v. 48), that all the honour which will be given to her from that day forward through all generations is not really hers. She only shines forth the greatness of God, her Saviour (vv. 46-47). She rightly sees herself at the end of a long history of God's saving presence among his people, crushing the mighty and exalting the lowly (see vv. 50-55). 'The Almighty has done great things for me, holy is his name' (v. 49).

The Feast of the Assumption is further recognition from the Church that the Almighty has done great things for his lowly handmaiden. It is an expression of hope that God will continue to do such great things for the rest of humankind. Mary lived a life believing that the promise made to her by the Lord would be fulfilled. Her generous and never-failing trust and faith in God's word led to this final word: she is taken to be with him forever. The meaning of today's Feast is aptly summarised by the liturgy itself: 'Today the Virgin Mother of God was taken up into heaven to be the beginning and the pattern of the Church in its perfection, and a sign of hope and comfort for your people on their pilgrim way' *(Preface of the Assumption)*.

THE TRIUMPH OF THE CROSS

John 3:13-17

The Son of Man must be lifted up

The early Christians faced the scandal of Jesus' death realistically. The historical reality of the cruel death of Jesus could not be sidestepped. Christians had to live their lives in the light of the Cross, and they had to preach the message of the Cross, 'to the Jews an obstacle that they cannot get over, to the pagans madness' (1 Cor 1:24). The Liturgy continues to preach the Cross. The suffering of Jesus crucified lies at the heart of the celebrations of Good Friday, but the Cross was not only the instrument used for the death of Jesus. It is also the sign of Jesus' unconditional response to God and is, therefore, his moment of triumph.

God created all things, but creation, with humankind at its centre, rebelled and tried to make its own way, without God. Humankind wanders, lost in a wilderness, not knowing or understanding its creating and loving God. No one from earth is able to ascend to God's presence, in order to regain knowledge and understanding of the very purpose for our existence (Jn 3:13).

However, someone has come down: Jesus, 'the Son of Man' (v. 13). Once Jesus is among us he takes to himself the task of making his Father known, and he does this by being 'lifted up' on a stake, just as Moses had 'lifted up' the serpent in the wilderness (v. 14). All the Israelites were cured of their ailments when they gazed upon the elevated serpent (Num 21:8-9). Anyone who believes that a God of love can be seen by gazing upon the elevated Son of Man will have eternal life (Jn 3:14-15). The logic behind this simple process depends upon one single fact: 'God loved the world so much that he gave his only son so that everyone who believes in him may not be lost but may have eternal life' (v. 16).

The Cross is not only an instrument of torture and death. It is also the place where our God, who is love itself (see 1 Jn 4:8, 16), makes himself known to us. The only way to make love known is to perform loving deeds. As Jesus himself taught: 'A man can have no greater love than to lay down his life for his friends' (Jn 15:13). We rightly say to those we love: 'Don't just tell me that you love me — show me!' The words 'I love you' have been cheapened so much. True love must do more than say words. Jesus makes the love of God known to us through all his life and teaching, but his supreme act of love is his final 'Yes' to his Father, as he is lifted up from the earth on the Cross. The Cross is the place where we see how much God loves us, and where we see how much Jesus loved his Father.

The Cross will always play an important part in the Christian life. There are two ways of looking at the Cross. On the one hand it guides us towards the light and hope of risen life when we are in the darkness, but it must also be seen as the answer to the question which we at times pose: 'How much does God love me?' The crucifix is the answer: no person can have greater love than this. At the end of its story of Jesus' passion, the Gospel of John makes a comment which we must all take to heart: 'They will look on the one whom they have pierced' (19:37). There we can discover the triumph of Jesus who has shown us how much God loves us, and how much he wants us to love in return: 'Love one another, *as I have loved you*' (13:34).

ALL SAINTS

Matthew 5:1-12

A program for holiness

There are the widely-acclaimed 'Saints', and there are 'saints'. The Church recognises the ranks of holy people, those written with a small letter who have unspectacularly loved and served God in the way of Jesus Christ. Although the major part of the liturgical interest in the holy ones from the history of Christianity is focused upon the great women and men of our past, the 'Saints', today we celebrate a major Feast in honour of the 'saints'. The Gospel text, the Beatitudes from the Gospel of Matthew, both tells of the way already chosen by those we honour, and challenges all who would like to join these saints.

As once the Law was given to Moses on the mountain of Sinai, now the new and perfect Moses, Jesus, gathers a new people of God, his disciples, on a mountain to give them a new Law. Jesus tells his disciples that they have been blessed (our lectionary's 'happy' is too tame) in a particular way if their lives have certain qualities. To be gentle, to mourn, to thirst for what is right, to be merciful, pure in heart and a peacemaker are the signs of the presence of the kingdom of God in our lives. We do not acquire these qualities simply by our own will-power and hard work. We receive them from a loving God, if we are prepared to abandon our way to happiness, and accept his way. Sanctity is not something we acquire by our own efforts. It is a gift God offers to us and we are free to accept or refuse this gift.

God gifts us with the virtues that proclaim his presence in our lives. There are four qualities in the Christian life which show our receptivity to the goodness of God: poverty of spirit, gentleness, a preparedness to mourn and a hunger for justice. Then there are four further qualities which demonstrate our preparedness to actively work for the extension of God's kingdom: the gift of mercy, a single-minded commitment to the ways of God, without any ambiguity (purity of heart is not about one's sexual situation . . . even though it would follow from a commitment to the ways of God), a preparedness to create peace around us and a willingness to love the Lord, cost us what it may.

Jesus concludes by speaking to the experience of the Church. As, in the name of Jesus, we stand over against the arrogant secularism which has pushed Christianity to the peripheries of our contemporary society and culture, a form of persecution and calumny are a part of our every day experience. To live this situation reflecting the blessedness which flows from the gifts of God, merits the final gift of his never-ending presence to us.

The Feast of All Saints is closely linked to the Commemoration of the Faithful Departed. What we have and what we are today comes from the gifts, both material and spiritual, which we have been given through the love and service of those who went before us. Today the Church calls us to praise God for raising up the saints we have known, and to ask for his continued gifts that we too may grow in holiness.

ALL SOULS*

John 11:17-27

Do you believe this?

After some delay (see Jn 11:5-7) Jesus goes to a town called Bethany where his friend Lazarus has died. Bethany is a town very close to Jerusalem, and Lazarus lived there with his two sisters, Martha and Mary. People from Jerusalem have gathered in Bethany. But Lazarus has already been in the tomb four days (Jn 11:17-18). The events which follow may happen in Bethany, but Jerusalem and people from Jerusalem are close at hand. This is preparation for the events which will soon take place during the Passover in Jerusalem (see 11:55-57).

Martha goes out to meet Jesus, reprimanding him for not coming to her brother when he was in need. There are many levels of human expression found in her words, which so often are matched by our own approach to God in our times of trouble. On the one hand she is disappointed that Jesus did not enter their story earlier, so that Lazarus might not have died (v. 21). Yet, her disappointment is matched by her belief that if he had come in time, he would have been able to help (v. 22).

Once Jesus enters into dialogue with Martha, the discussion becomes double edged. He opens the discussion by baldly stating that Lazarus would rise again (v. 23). Martha is aware of this, as she accepts the widespread, although not universal, idea that there will be a life after death (v. 24). She has not understood what Jesus is

* The Lectionary offers three series of readings for this celebration. I will comment on the third series, where the Gospel of John is used.

promising her. She is working within categories which come to her from her Jewish background and culture. Jesus is promising more.

Resurrection and life are available now, because Jesus is the resurrection. Anyone who believes in Jesus already has life (vv. 25-26). It does not matter if a person's human story comes to an end; belief in Jesus gives us life both in the now and in the hereafter. 'Whoever lives and believes in me will never die' (v. 26). When asked if she believes in this, Martha makes a confession of faith: 'I believe that you are the Christ, the Son of God, the one who was to come into this world' (v. 27).

We all share that belief, but Martha still has not fully understood Jesus' promise of life. The terms 'the Christ', 'the Son of God', 'the one who was to come into this world' still come to her from her Jewish culture and background. These three expressions formed part of first century Jewish messianic hopes. They are correct when they are applied to Jesus, but Jesus is more than the fulfilment of Jewish messianic hopes.

Martha struggles to understand that Jesus' promises outstrip our dreams. As we look back over the story of our loved ones, the ones whose life, love and death have given us our own life and possibilities, we are asked to recognise that there is no human hope that can totally satisfy us. Martha accepts Jesus from within her religion and culture. She tries to fit him into her way of seeing things. We all do the same. Death is the most wonderful sign to us all that such an approach to Jesus falls short of the mark. He has more to offer us than our hopes. He asks us to believe in him so that we may have life, both now and forever.

DEDICATION OF THE LATERAN BASILICA

John 2:13-22

My Father's house

The Church belongs to this world. It is made up of people who live, love and worship. For this reason the holy places we have come to know as 'Churches' are honoured. One of those Churches — the Church of St. John Lateran in Rome — is honoured in the universal calendar of the Roman tradition because it is the 'Mother and Head of all Churches of the City and the World'. It is accorded this honour because it was the first Christian basilica, constructed on the Lateran Hill in Rome, by the Emperor Constantine. The Gospel story of Jesus' concern for his Father's House fittingly marks the celebration.

Yet, as always in the Gospel, the story has many surprises. Jesus drives out of the Temple the very people who are necessary for the cult which took place there. It was essential for entry into the Temple to change all coins into Tyrian coinage, and anyone who wished to offer sacrifice needed to have animals — larger beasts for the wealthy, or pigeons for the poorer people (Jn 2:15-16). Jesus is not only angry because of the commerce which is being conducted in the Temple. Something more important is happening. Jesus is bringing old established and, in some ways, necessary practices to an end because the Temple is no longer simply a place of cult. Jesus proclaims the Temple as 'my Father's house' (v. 16).

This leads the disciples to think of the great heroes of Israel, especially of the immediate past during the Maccabean revolt (during the 160's B.C.), when people gave their lives for the Temple. They think they understand

Jesus's action in terms of the words of the Psalm: 'Zeal for your house will devour me' (v. 17). At least they are aware that such a passionate love for the things of his Father will eventually lead to Jesus' death, but there is more at stake which they have not yet grasped.

Asked for some sign which authorises his actions, Jesus tells 'the Jews': 'Destroy this sanctuary, and in three days I will raise it up' (v. 19). But they take his words, and throw them back at him: 'Are you going to raise it up in three days?' (v. 20). They are unable to see beyond their own achievements of building the Temple of wood and stone. Like the disciples, they still have a great deal to learn. However, they have erred more seriously than the disciples. They have taken the very words of Jesus — and rejected them.

Living in the Church, we are aware that Jesus is more than a passionate devotee of the ancient Jewish Temple or a reformer who will replace a corrupt Temple. He is the living Temple of God among us: 'He was speaking of the sanctuary that was his body' (v. 21). After his resurrection his own disciples came to appreciate his presence among them: they believed the scripture and the words he had said (v. 22).

Both in the celebration of Eucharist and in the self-giving of our eucharistic lives we draw from Jesus, alive among us in the scriptures and in the words which he spoke. On the day when we recall the foundation of the Mother of all Churches, we have reason to recall gratefully that it is within 'the Church' that the Scriptures, Word of the risen Jesus, are made available to us.

SOME FURTHER READING

Commentaries on Matthew's Gospel

Beare, F.W., *The Gospel according to Matthew. A Commentary* (Oxford: Basil Blackwell, 1981). A single-volumed but extensive commentary. Reliable, but better in some sections of the Gospel than others.

Davies, W.D. - Allison, D.C., *The Gospel According to Saint Matthew* (International Critical Commentary; Edinburgh, T. & T. Clark, 1988, 1991-). There are now two published volumes (covering an introduction and Mt 1-18) of a planned three-volumed commentary. Davies and Allison have produced a classical commentary of the highest order. Not a stone is left unturned to approach all the historical, philological, religious and theological possibilities of the Matthean text. This is a wonderful work.

Fenton, J.C., *Saint Matthew* (The Pelican New Testament Commentaries; Harmondsworth: Penguin Books, 1963). Although published nearly 30 years ago, and thus not aware of many recent debates, this brief commentary is still an accurate guide to a reading of Matthew.

Harrington, D.J., *The Gospel of Matthew* (Sacra Pagina 1; Collegeville: Michael Glazier/Liturgical Press, 1991). This is the first volume of a promising new series. Harrington does excellent work on historical and philological questions, and the commentary is reliable on those issues. Its strengths do not lie in the theological reading of the Gospel. It may not be of immediate help to the preacher, but is a rich resource for the background to Matthew.

Hill, D., *The Gospel of Matthew* (New Century Bible; London: Oliphants, 1972). A good single volume commentary. It is now, unfortunately, a little out of touch with some of the modern discussions, but still guides the reader expertly through the Matthean text.

Gundry, R.H., *Matthew. A Commentary on his Literary and Theological Art* (Grand Rapids: Eerdmans, 1982). This book comes from a scholar from an evangelical tradition, but it is outstanding in its attempt to read the theological and structural unity of the Gospel of Matthew. At times Gundry's attempt to keep his foot in both camps (historical exegesis and the theological possibilities of the text) leads to 'maverick' positions. The book is nevertheless full of rich insights.

Luz, U., *Matthew 1-7. A Commentary* (Edinburgh: T. & T. Clark, 1989-). This is the first volume of another proposed three-volume commentary. Although very different from Davies-Allison, it also promises to be a first rate work. Luz devotes less space to the more traditional exegetical questions (although they are all covered), and pays particular attention to the way in which the Christian tradition has used the Gospel of Matthew.

Meier, J.P., *Matthew* (New Testament Message; Wilmington: Michael Glazier, 1980). The best of the single volume commentaries. Although Meier still follows the older idea of Matthew's Gospel being structured around five 'books', his treatment of each single passage is profound yet marked by a lightness of touch and good pastoral sense.

Patte, D., *The Gospel According to Matthew. A Structural Commentary on Matthew's Faith* (Philadelphia: Fortress Press, 1987). Patte has been the main advocate of structuralism in English-speaking biblical studies. Yet this commentary does not suffer from some of the difficult jargon which has emerged from structuralism. It is a 'different' commentary, as Patte strives to make sense of the Gospel as a whole, single statement of faith, addressed to a reader. It is a stimulating — if at times different — study of the Gospel.

Schweizer, E., *The Good News according to Matthew* (London: SPCK, 1975). Another excellent one volume commentary, blending the detailed study of the text with some useful pastoral and theological applications.

Viviano, B.T., 'The Gospel According to Matthew', in R.E. Brown - J.A. Fitzmyer - R.E. Murphy (eds.), *The New Jerome Biblical Commentary* (Englewood Cliffs: Prentice Hall, 1990) pp. 630-674. This study offers an introduction to the Gospel of Matthew, a brief commentary on each section of the text. Up to date further bibliographical references are added to each section of the introduction and the commentary.

Other books on Matthew's Gospel

Bauer, D.R., *The Structure of Matthew's Gospel. A Study in Literary Design* (Journal for the Study of the New Testament Supplement Series 31; Sheffield: Almond Press, 1989).

Bornkamm, G. - Barth, G. - Held, H.-J., *Tradition and Interpretation in Matthew* (London: SCM Press, 1982). Second Edition.

Brown, R.E., *The Birth of the Messiah. A Commentary on the Infancy Narratives in Matthew and Luke* (Garden City: Doubleday, 1977) pp. 43-232.

Brown, R.E., *The Churches the Apostles Left Behind* (New York: Paulist Press, 1984).

Brown, R.E. - Meier, J.P., *Antioch and Rome. New Testament Cradles of Catholic Christianity* (New York: Paulist Press, 1983).

Doohan, L., *Matthew. Spirituality for the '80s and '90s* (Santa Fe: Bear & Company, 1985).

Edwards, R.A., *Matthew's Story of Jesus* (Philadelphia: Fortress Press, 1985).

Kingsbury, J.D., *Matthew. A Commentary for Preachers and Others* (London: SPCK, 1977).

Kingsbury, J.D., *Matthew as Story* (Philadelphia: Fortress Press, 1988). Second Edition.

Kingsbury, J.D., *Matthew: Structure, Christology, Kingdom* (Philadelphia: Fortress Press, 1975).

Lambrecht, J., *The Sermon on the Mount. Proclamation and Exhortation* (Good News Studies 14; Wilmington: Michael Glazier, 1985).

McGinlay, H. (ed.), *The Year of Matthew* (Melbourne: Desbooks/ J.B.C.E., 1983).

Matera, F.J., 'The Plot of Matthew's Gospel', *The Catholic Biblical Quarterly* 49 (1987) 233-253.

Meier, J.P., *The Vision of Matthew. Christ, Church and Morality in the First Gospel* (Theological Inquiries; New York: Paulist Press, 1979).

Moloney, F.J., *A Body Broken for a Broken People. Eucharist in the New Testament* (Melbourne: Collins Dove, 1990) pp. 36-53.

Moloney, F.J., *The Living Voice of the Gospel. The Gospels Today* (Melbourne: Collins Dove, 1986) pp. 115-158.

Senior, D., *What are they saying about Matthew?* (New York: Paulist Press, 1983).

Senior, D., *The Passion of Jesus in the Gospel of Matthew* (The Passion Series 1; Wilmington: Michael Glazier, 1985).

Stanton, G., *The Gospels and Jesus* (The Oxford Bible Series; Oxford: University Press, 1989) pp. 59-80.

Stanton, G. (ed.), *The Interpretation of Matthew* (Issues in Religion and Theology 3; London: SPCK, 1983).

INDEX OF GOSPEL PASSAGES

The following passages are listed according to the order of their appearance in the Gospels to aid readers who wish to use this book on the occasions throughout any Liturgical Year when these Readings are used outside the Year A Sunday Cycle. Some may also like to use the book for personal reflection on a favourite Gospel story and may turn to the index to locate a reflection upon that passage. I have only indexed the Gospel Readings which have a full commentary. Thus, not every citation from the Gospels mentioned in the book is listed here.

Page	Gospel of Luke
208	1:39-56
202	1:5-17,66-80
72	2:1-14
78	2:16-21
200	2:22-40
114	24:13-35

Page	Gospel of John
74	1:1-18
132	1:29-34
216	2:13-22
210	3:13-17
128	3:16-18
90	4:5-42
130	6:51-58
92	9:1-41
116	10:1-10
94	11:1-45
214	11:17-27
118	14:1-12
120	14:15-21
110	20:1-9
112	20:19-23
124	20:19-31